THE
COMPLETE
BIBLE QUIZ
BOOK

THE COMPLETE BIBLE QUIZ BOOK

Dan Carlinsky

WINGS BOOKS
New York

This 1999 edition is published by Wings Books,®
an imprint of Random House Value Publishing, Inc.,
201 East 50th Street, New York, New York 10022.

Wings Books® and design are registered trademarks of
Random House Value Publishing, Inc.

Random House
New York • Toronto • London • Sydney • Auckland
http://www.randomhouse.com/

Printed and bound in the United States of America

Library of Congress Cataloging-in-Publication Data
Carlinsky, Dan.
The complete Bible quiz book.
1. Bible—Examinations, questions, etc. I. Title.
BS612.C35   1985   220'.076   77-78125
ISBN 0-517-23278-2

37 36 35 34 33 32 31

The Quizzes

* Denotes quiz especially for beginners

1. Titles

These titles don't appear anywhere in the Bible, but if you've read the stories you should know in a jiffy what characters could have claimed them.

1. "The Giant Killer"

2. "The Lion Tamer"

3. "The Strong Man"

4. "The Wise King"

5. "Mr. Patience"

2. Complete the Quote

6. "And she brought forth her first-born son, and wrapped him in swaddling clothes, and laid him in a manger; because..."

7. "MENE, MENE,..."

8. "Cast thy bread upon the waters:..."

9. "I am the bread of life: he that cometh to me shall never hunger;..."

10. "Heal me, O Lord, and I shall be healed;..."

11. "If thine enemy hunger, _____ _____; if he thirst, _____ _____ _____."

12. "O death, where is thy sting?..."

2

13. "For where two or three are gathered together in my name..."

14. "Neither do I condemn thee;..."

15. "For unto us a child is born, unto us a..."

16. "Thy word is a lamp unto my feet, and..."

17. "If God be for us,..."

18. "Whither thou goest, I will go; and..."

19. "And ye shall know the truth, and the truth shall..."

20. "For many are called..."

3. Multiple Choice—The Easy Test

Pick one of four in each of these questions. Not too tough.

21. The robe Jesus wore as the Roman soldiers taunted him was—
    A. scarlet or purple
    B. red
    C. many coloured
    D. black

22. According to Proverbs, the beginning of knowledge is—
    A. fear of the Lord
    B. knowledge of the Lord
    C. knowledge of thyself
    D. concern for all mankind

23. "The living know that they shall die," but what do the dead know?
    A. "that they shall be reborn"
    B. "the presence of God"
    C. "what the living knoweth not"
    D. "not any thing"

24. Judas indicated to the crowd who Jesus was by—
    A. pointing to him
    B. kissing him
    C. kicking him
    D. laying figs at his feet

25. "There is no peace, saith my God, to the _____."
    A. warriors
    B. wicked
    C. weary
    D. Israelites

26. What was king Belshazzar doing when the Handwriting on the Wall appeared?
    A. praying
    B. waging war
    C. drinking
    D. writing

27. Jonah—
    A. was cast into the sea by a drunken heathen
    B. was cast into the sea by the crew of his ship
    C. fell into the sea while looking for land
    D. ended up in the sea after his ship capsized

28. When Ezekiel was in the valley of dry bones, he watched as the Lord brought the bones together, gave them sinews and flesh, and covered them with skin.

What was missing and how did Ezekiel supply it?
- A. hair; he wove it of the rays of golden sun
- B. breath; he called it from the four winds
- C. souls; he prayed to God to give them souls
- D. blood; he closed his eyes and passed his hands over them

29. After David downed Goliath with a stone from his sling, he—
- A. cut off his head with his sword
- B. cut off his head with Goliath's own sword
- C. cut off his head with a sword borrowed from one of his brothers
- D. cut off both his giant hands and brought them back to camp

30. What happened at the rock of Horeb?
- A. Joshua was buried
- B. Moses struck the rock and produced water
- C. a crowd was converted to the faith of Moses
- D. Jesus spoke to three women

31. Lot's wife looked back at the burning city of Sodom and became a pillar of salt. But Lot escaped with—
- A. his two daughters
- B. his son and daughter
- C. his two sons and two daughters
- D. his belongings

32. Esau was the hairy brother, but what color was his complexion?
- A. pale
- B. red
- C. dark brown
- D. light brown

33. Who was renamed Israel? Was it—
    A. Abraham
    B. Isaac
    C. Jacob
    D. Mordecai

34. God told Noah to make an ark of—
    A. pine
    B. birch
    C. cedar
    D. gopher wood

35. How long was Lazarus in the tomb?
    A. four days
    B. four hours
    C. one week
    D. two days

36. How was Abraham going to kill his son Isaac in sacrifice?
    A. slay him with a knife
    B. drown him in the river Jordan
    C. drown him in the Red Sea
    D. throw him off Mount Sinai

37. The Lord told Adam that if he ate of the tree of knowledge of good and evil he would—
    A. be banished from the Garden of Eden
    B. never see Eve again
    C. go blind
    D. die

38. What was the first thing Noah did upon leaving the ark?
    A. looked for the dove
    B. bent both his knees

C. lectured his sons on self-reliance
D. built an altar

39. How many books are in the Testaments, New and Old,
King James Version?
   A. thirty-nine
   B. forty-nine
   C. sixty-six
   D. one hundred

40. Luke was called—
   A. "the revered Greek"
   B. "the scholarly saint"
   C. "the beloved physician"
   D. "the sympathetic evangelist"

4. True or False?

Fifteen statements about Old Testament tales. Answer each with "true" or "false."

41. Delilah cut Samson's hair. True or false?

42. Before being cast into the sea, Jonah begged for time to say his prayers. True or false?

43. The Lord parted the sea for Moses and the Israelites by producing a great fish that swallowed up the water. True or false?

44. God performed a miracle similar to the parting of the Red Sea at the Jordan River. True or false?

45. The sound of the trumpets and rams' horns immediately preceded the tumbling of the wall of Jericho. True or false?

46. When Joshua was fighting in Canaan, the sun stood still in the sky for forty days and forty nights. True or false?

47. Moses died on Mount Nebo, in the land of Moab, unprepared for death because the Lord had not seen fit to forewarn him. True or false?

48. Joseph was not the only Biblical character with a garment of many colours. The virgin daughters of King David also wore such clothing. True or false?

49. Solomon's temple was so grand that it was described as being larger by far than Noah's ark. True or false?

50. Elijah went to heaven on the back of a golden mule. True or false?

51. Job died shortly after his trials and tribulations. True or false?

52. Darius, ruler of Babylon, had Daniel thrown into the lions' den because he resented Daniel's praying to God. True or false?

53. According to the laws of Deuteronomy, it's all right to eat your neighbor's grapes, as long as you don't put any into a container. Similarly, it is permissible to pick someone else's corn as long as it's done by hand. True or false?

54. Nebuchadnezzar threw Shadrach, Meshach, and Abednego into a fiery furnace for refusing to bow down and worship an idol, but they were unharmed by the fire. True or false?

55. According to the book of Proverbs, "The fear of the Lord is the beginning of knowledge." True or false?

5. Dreams

Everybody dreams, Biblical characters not excepted. Join the dreamer with the subject of his night-time fantasies.

56. A ladder   Joseph

57. Cows and corn   Jacob

58. An image with head of gold, arms   Abimelech
    of silver, and belly of brass

59. The sun, moon, and stars all   Pharoah
    making obeisance to him

60. God telling him to give Sarah back   Nebuchadnezzar
    to Abraham

6. Moses

Prophet, leader of the Jewish people, great lawgiver, Moses is a towering figure of the Old Testament. Here are ten questions on his life, his words, and his deeds.

61. Moses, as a newborn infant, was hidden near the river for three months. True or false?

62. Who was paid wages for nursing Moses?

63. The count of men led out of Egypt by Moses is put at—
    A. 60,000
    B. 600,000
    C. 6,000,000
    D. 6,000

64. What was the weather like the day God gave Moses the Ten Commandments?

A. sunny
B. rainy
C. thundering and lightning
D. the Bible does not say

65. God gave Moses the Ten Commandments twice. True or false?

66. Complete this prayer of Moses': "Rise up, Lord, and let thine enemies be scattered; and let them that hate thee _____ _____ _____."

67. Why weren't Moses and Aaron allowed to enter the Promised Land?
    A. they had promoted much murmuring among the people
    B. they took the name of the Lord in vain
    C. they spoke of it with too much longing and desire
    D. they took credit for bringing water out of the rock

68. What did Moses tell the people to give as an offering when they reached the Promised Land?
    A. a basket of "the first of all the fruit of the earth"
    B. a basket of "figs and grapes and melons ripe"
    C. "a young lamb, shorn of its covering to God and anointed with oil"
    D. "whatsoever ye hold most dear"

69. Complete this quotation from Deuteronomy: "The Lord thy God will raise up unto thee a Prophet, from the midst of thee, of thy brethren, like unto me; unto him _____ _____ _____."

70. Where did the Lord bury Moses?

7. What Book Does It Come From?

71. The burning bush.
   - A. Genesis
   - B. Exodus
   - C. Leviticus
   - D. Deuteronomy

72. "Blessed are the meek: for they shall inherit the earth."
   - A. Mark
   - B. Matthew
   - C. Acts
   - D. Revelation

73. "God is Love."
   - A. 1 John
   - B. Genesis
   - C. Matthew
   - D. Job

74. "He was received up into heaven, and sat on the right hand of God."
    A. Mark
    B. Luke
    C. Colossians
    D. 2 Thessalonians

75. "Dust thou art and unto dust shalt thou return."
    A. Deuteronomy
    B. Ecclesiastes
    C. Genesis
    D. Exodus

76. "At the name of Jesus every knee should bow...."
    A. John
    B. Galatians
    C. Hebrews
    D. Philippians

77. "For God so loved the world, that he gave his only begotten Son, that whosoever believeth in him should not perish, but have everlasting life."
    A. John
    B. Titus
    C. 2 Peter
    D. Jude

78. "I am the living bread which came down from heaven; if any man eat of this bread, he shall live for ever."
    A. Matthew
    B. Acts
    C. Isaiah
    D. John

79. The Ten Commandments.
    A. Genesis

B. Numbers
C. Leviticus
D. Exodus

80. The laws of clean eating.
    A. Ecclesiastes
    B. Joshua
    C. Leviticus
    D. Malachi

81. "Cursed be he that maketh the blind to wander out of the way. And all the people shall say, Amen."
    A. Matthew
    B. Mark
    C. Esther
    D. Deuteronomy

82. The story of the olive tree, the fig tree, the vine, and the bramble.
    A. John
    B. Luke
    C. Judges
    D. Ruth

83. "There is no new thing under the sun."
    A. Genesis
    B. Exodus
    C. Ezekiel
    D. Ecclesiastes

84. An outline of the qualities of a virtuous woman, she whose "price is far above rubies."
    A. Esther
    B. Proverbs
    C. Psalms
    D. James

16

85. Jesus' giving himself up by announcing twice, "I am he."
    A. Luke
    B. Acts
    C. John
    D. Galatians

86. The ark of God is placed next to the Philistines' idol, Dagon; Dagon falls on his face.
    A. 1 Kings
    B. 1 Samuel
    C. 1 Chronicles
    D. 2 Chronicles

87. David tells Solomon to build a temple as he had wanted to do.
    A. 2 Kings
    B. 1 Samuel
    C. 1 Chronicles
    D. 2 Chronicles

88. "Behold, a virgin shall conceive, and bear a son, and shall call his name Immanuel."
    A. Isaiah
    B. Zechariah
    C. Malachi
    D. Mark

89. "The son shall not bear the iniquity of the father, neither shall the father bear the iniquity of the son."
    A. Ezekiel
    B. Judges
    C. Proverbs
    D. Psalms

90. "God is jealous, and the Lord revengeth; the Lord revengeth, and is furious: the Lord will take vengeance

on his adversaries, and he reserveth wrath for his enemies."
    A. Job.
    B. Daniel
    C. Nahum
    D. Romans

91. "And a little child shall lead them."
    A. Haggai
    B. Isaiah
    C. Lamentations
    D. 2 John

92. "Can the Ethiopian change his skin, or the leopard his spots?"
    A. Genesis
    B. Ezra
    C. Hosea
    D. Jeremiah

93. Paul's listing of the "works of the flesh" and the "fruit of the Spirit."
    A. Galatians
    B. Acts
    C. Ephesians
    D. 1 Corinthians

94. "If it be possible, as much as lieth in you, live peaceably with all men."
    A. Exodus
    B. Matthew
    C. Romans
    D. Solomon's Song

95. "Children, obey your parents in the Lord."
    A. Ephesians
    B. Exodus
    C. Numbers
    D. Luke

8. Places

Do you know your Bible geography? Here's a quiz to test your recall of Biblical locations. Start with this short matching quiz on five mountains.

96. Where Moses received the law. Hor

97. Where the Lord showed Moses "all the land of Gilead"—The Promised Land. Ararat

98. Where Aaron died. Sinai

99. Where God told Abraham to take Isaac for the sacrifice. Moriah

100. Where Noah's ark came to rest. Nebo

101. Give the birthplace of Saul (later called Paul).

102. For what was the land of Shinar famous in Genesis?

103. Where in the plains of Jericho did Joshua and the Israelites keep the passover? G __ __ __ __ __.

104. When Joshua divided the land of Canaan, he gave to Caleb the place called _____.

105. As Jesus sat on Jacob's well, a woman came to draw water. "Give me to drink," Jesus said to her. Where did this take place?

106. Where did King Ahasuerus reside?
    A. Shushan
    B. Shechem
    C. Shochoh
    D. Gilead

107. What isle was visited by John? P __ __ __ __ __.

108. Where did Jesus raise Lazarus from the dead? B __ __ __ __ __ __.

109. Job was of the land of _____.

110. Where did the Lord send Jonah to convert the populace?
    A. Tyrus
    B. Egypt
    C. "across the sea"
    D. Nineveh

111. The bones of Joseph were buried in—
    A. Gaza
    B. Shechem

21

C. Kadesh

D. Jerusalem

112. After being at sea in a terrible storm, Paul was shipwrecked on the isle of M _ _ _ _ _.

113. What piece of land did the chief priests buy with thirty pieces of silver at the time of Jesus' trial?

114. Matthew, Mark, and John call it Golgotha, the place of a skull, but Luke calls it _____.

115. "Then Philip went down to the city of _____, and preached Christ unto them."
   A. Damascus
   B. Samaria
   C. Bethlehem
   D. Galilee

116. Where did Saul see the vision that led to his conversion?

117. When the messengers from Cornelius went to speak with Simon Peter, they found him praying. Where?

118. Where were the disciples first called Christians? At A _ _ _ _ _ _.

119. Where did John the Baptist first baptize people?

120. Where did Jesus say he had seen Nathaniel before?

121. Name the pool, near the sheep market at Jerusalem, at which Jesus cured the impotent man. B _ _ _ _ _ _ _.

122. Jesus said, instead of praying in public so that everyone sees, "thou, when thou prayest, enter into _____ _____."

123. When Jesus delivered the parables by the sea, where was he and where was his audience?

124. Jesus was arrested in the garden at G ___ ___ ___ ___ ___ ___ ___ ___.

125. Where did David slay Goliath?

126. Isaiah predicted this city would become "a ruinous heap": D ___ ___ ___ ___ ___ ___ ___.

127. Jeremiah quoted the Lord as promising that Jerusalem would be dominated by this country for seventy years; then the country would be destroyed. What country? B ___ ___ ___ ___ ___ ___.

128. The Book of Ezekiel opens with the prophet in exile in the land of the Chaldeans, near the river C ___ ___ ___ ___ ___.

129. Where was it that Shadrach, Meshach, and Abednego refused to bow to a golden image, angering Nebuchadnezzar to such degree that he had them thrown into a burning, fiery furnace? Was it—
   A. the plain of Dura, in the province of Babylon
   B. mount Nebo
   C. at the border of Damascus
   D. at a crossroads

130. Where did Cain go when he left Eden, heading east?

23

9. All in the Family

Fifteen quick questions and a matching quiz—all asking who was related to whom.

131. Who was Solomon's father? His mother?

132. What Old Testament villain was the son of Hammedatha the Agagite?

133. Who was Jesse?

134. Was Irad Adam's grandson or great-grandson?

135. Who was Methuselah's most famous grandson?

136. What relation was Lot to Abraham?

137. Were Abraham's brother Nahor's two eldest sons
named—
   A. Huz and Buz
   B. Huz and Muz
   C. Fuz and Suz
   D. Luz and Shuz

138. What relation was Jacob to Laban?

139. Esther and Mordecai were _____.

140. Naomi met a man in Bethlehem called Boaz, who was a
relative of _____.

141. Jochebed was two things to Moses. What two?

142. What relations of Lazarus called Jesus to his side?

143. In Lystra, Paul met "a certain disciple" named
Timotheus, whose mother was a Jewess but whose
father was a _____.

144. David was so taken with Bathsheba's looks that he
arranged for the battle death of her husband,
U __ __ __ __.

145. Whom did Jesus declare to be "my brother, and my
sister, and mother"?

Now match:

146. Laban's daughter   Saul

147. David's father-in-law   Joash

148. Jonah's father   Rachel

149. Gideon's father   Enoch

150. Cain's firstborn   Amittai

10. Hidden Words—Women

151-185. If your eye is sharp, you'll find the names of thirty-five Biblical women buried in the maze of letters. The names run up and down, left and right, diagonally, forward and backward—but always in a straight line.

A	C	H	L	N	A	O	M	I	S	M	A	I	R	I	M	H
B	C	R	T	R	D	I	V	I	V	E	X	A	N	P	L	T
I	O	H	E	U	I	N	I	B	N	R	V	J	Q	O	J	I
G	D	A	J	M	R	L	E	H	C	A	R	E	K	R	A	D
A	N	N	A	E	O	J	A	Z	G	B	E	Z	F	A	S	U
I	Q	U	H	Y	K	G	H	I	D	E	B	E	H	C	O	J
L	O	T	O	W	A	Z	T	D	A	F	E	B	A	G	U	V
D	S	A	L	R	V	I	V	E	A	B	K	E	N	E	R	F
E	R	B	A	H	O	L	I	B	A	H	A	L	N	J	O	O
M	K	I	H	H	A	P	R	O	C	T	A	D	A	P	N	S
A	M	T	E	E	N	A	M	R	L	A	L	E	H	K	L	R
R	B	H	S	B	L	H	O	A	M	M	L	D	L	P	A	O
Y	Z	A	S	H	U	A	H	H	N	E	C	O	U	M	H	H
L	X	S	A	I	D	O	R	E	H	H	B	V	A	R	C	E
H	A	R	U	T	E	K	J	V	A	S	H	T	I	V	I	T
W	A	S	P	O	O	C	I	H	L	A	H	T	R	A	M	H
S	P	E	N	I	N	N	A	H	T	B	M	O	Y	O	K	R

27

11. Who Said...?

186. "For the wages of sin is death...."

187. "No prophet is accepted in his own country."

188. "By their fruits ye shall know them."

189. "What hath God wrought!"

190. "Divide the living child in two, and give half to the one, and half to the other."

191. "And now, behold, the king walketh before you; and I am old and grayheaded...."

192. "There is none holy as the Lord: for there is none beside thee: neither is there any rock like our God."

193. "Repent ye: for the kingdom of heaven is at hand."

194. "For I am now ready to be offered, and the time of my departure is at hand. I have fought a good fight, I have finished my course, I have kept the faith."

195. "The Lord gave, and the Lord hath taken away; blessed be the name of the Lord."

196. "For the Lord himself shall descend from heaven with a shout, with the voice of the archangel, and with the trump of God: and the dead in Christ shall rise first: Then we which are alive and remain, shall be caught up together with them in the clouds, to meet the Lord in the air: and so shall we ever be with the Lord."

197. "Let us now go even unto Bethlehem, and see this thing which is come to pass, which the Lord hath made known unto us."

198. "When I was a child, I spake as a child, I understood as a child, I thought as a child; but when I became a man, I put away childish things."

199. "Peace, be still." (Spoken to stormy waters.)

200. "The Son of man is delivered into the hands of men, and they shall kill him; and after that he is killed, he shall risc the third day."

201. "Every son that is born ye shall cast into the river, and every daughter ye shall save alive."

202. "O my Lord, I am not eloquent, neither heretofore, nor since thou hast spoken unto thy servant: but I am slow of speech, and of a slow tongue."

203. "Who is on the Lord's side? Let him come unto me."

204. "Rabbi, thou art the Son of God; thou art the King of Israel."

205. "How doth the city sit solitary, that was full of people! how is she become as a widow! she that was great among the nations, and princess among the provinces, how is she become tributary!"

Now tell *to whom* it was said.

206. "Go in peace: and the God of Israel grant thee thy petition that thou hast asked of him." Spoken by Eli the priest.

207. "Silver and gold have I none; but such as I have give I thee; In the name of Jesus Christ of Nazareth, rise up and walk." Spoken by Peter.

208. "How can a man be born when he is old? can he enter the second time into his mother's womb, and be born?" Spoken by Nicodemus.

209. "Because thou hast mocked me: I would there were a sword in mine hand, for now would I kill thee." Spoken by Balaam.

210. "Loose thy shoe from off thy foot; for the place whereon thou standest is holy." Spoken by the captain of the host of the Lord.

And now, give both the speaker *and* the hearer.

211. "Am I my brother's keeper?"

212. "What will ye give me, and I will deliver him unto you?"

213. "If ye bring me home again to fight against the children of Ammon, and the Lord deliver them before me, shall I be your head?"

214. "And the swine, though he divide the hoof, and be clovenfooted, yet he cheweth not the cud; he is unclean to you."

215. "Hail, thou that art highly favoured, the Lord is with thee...."

Finally, tell *about* whom it was said.

216. "He hath Beelzebub, and by the prince of the devils casteth he out devils." Spoken by the scribes from Jerusalem.

217. "Would God I had died for thee...." Spoken by David.

218. "But now he is dead, wherefore should I fast? can I bring him back again? I shall go to him, but he shall not return to me." Spoken by David.

219. "How are the mighty fallen...!" Spoken by David.

220. "There is none like him in the earth, a perfect and an upright man, one that feareth God, and escheweth evil...." Spoken by the Lord to Satan.

12. Who's Who

Here some of the most important figures in the Bible are described in a single sentence. Can you name them from these single clues?

221. The Sabeans took his oxen and his asses, lightning killed his sheep, the Chaldeans stole his camels, his servants were killed, and his sons and daughters perished when a house collapsed.

222. He referred to Jesus as he "whose shoe's latchet I am not worthy to unloose."

223. He played his harp before the possessed King Saul and the evil spirit within the king left.

224. He "was wiser than all men; than Ethan the Ezrahite, and Heman, and Chalcol, and Darda, the sons of Mahol: and his fame was in all nations round about."

225. He took the people's golden earrings and fashioned them into a calf, which they worshipped.

226. Him "the Lord knew face to face."

227. He tried to steal the throne away from King David, his father.

228. He was ruler at the time of Jesus' birth, and it was his order that brought Joseph and Mary on the road to Bethlehem.

229. He walked on water—for a while—and then Jesus had to save him when he started to sink.

230. He had a vision in a whirlwind, of four living creatures: every one had four faces and four wings.

231. He took Abel's place.

232. He divided his three hundred men into three companies and gave each man a trumpet, an empty pitcher, and a lamp within the pitcher.

233. He was told that he would deny Jesus three times in one night.

234. He wrestled all night with a heavenly being.

235. He washed his hands in water, saying, "I am innocent of the blood of this just person."

236. These two were early foreign missionaries, sent to Salamis to teach the words of Jesus.

237. The prophet Agabus predicted that this man would be bound and delivered into the hands of the Gentiles at Jerusalem.

238. He replaced Moses as leader of the children of Israel after Moses died.

239. He interpreted the Handwriting on the Wall.

240. He walked naked and barefoot for three years.

13. It Didn't Happen

Which of the four choices is *not* applicable?

241. Which of the following *didn't* happen when Jesus died?
     A. dead saints rose from their graves
     B. the earth quaked
     C. the vail of the temple split in two
     D. the sun shone more brightly than ever before

242. What *didn't* happen on the day of the Pentecost?
     A. a rainbow filled the sky "from end to end"
     B. a sound like "a rushing mighty wind" filled the house
     C. "cloven tongues, like as of fire," hovered overhead
     D. the disciples spoke "with other tongues"

243. Which of the following *didn't* people think Jesus was?
    A. John the Baptist
    B. Elias
    C. one of the prophets
    D. Solomon

244. Which of the following is *not* spoken of in Ecclesiastes?
    A. a time to weep
    B. a time to sew
    C. a time to hate
    D. a time to pray

245. Which of the following did the sinner woman *not* do to Jesus as he sat eating in the house of Simon the Pharisee?
    A. wash his feet with her tears
    B. dry his feet with her hair
    C. speak to his feet as if unto a baby
    D. kiss his feet.

14. Husbands and Wives

Join up the spouses, all from the Old Testament.

246. Abraham   Ruth

247. Nahor   Sarah

248. Jacob   Rachel

249. Heber   Milcah

250. Boaz   Jael

15. Animals

From the first chapter of Genesis, when God made the living creatures of the sea, the air, and the land, animals of all sorts are mentioned throughout the Bible. Here are twenty questions from the Biblical zoo.

251. What kind of animal did Samson first tear apart barehanded at Timnath? Was it—
    A. a bear
    B. a lion
    C. a great fish
    D. a wolf

252. Saul was sent on an errand to seek his father's lost
    _____.

253. "Two hundred she goats, and twenty he goats, two hundred ewes and twenty rams, thirty milch camels with their colts, forty kine, and ten bulls, twenty she asses, and ten foals" combine to make a nice present. Who gave such a managerie to his brother?

254. What did Balaam's ass do that showed unusual talent for an animal?

255. In explaining his confidence in preparing to battle Goliath, what two animals did David boast of slaying while tending his father's sheep?

Isaiah spoke of a time to come when beasts would join together. Pick the animals from the right-hand column that would become friendly with those of the left.

256. The wolf will dwell with...   the bear

257. The leopard will lie down with...   the ox

258. The calf will join with...   the young lion

259. The cow will feed with...   the lamb

260. The lion will eat straw like...   the kid

261. What was Absalom riding when he was caught up in the branches of an oak tree?

262. According to Ecclesiastes, a living dog is better than what?

263. Jesus healed a possessed man by sending the demons into a great herd of _____.
    A. cows
    B. bulls
    C. swine
    D. buffalo

264. When he was warned against healing on the sabbath, Jesus asked, "What man shall there be among you that shall have one _____, and if it fall into a pit on the sabbath day, will he not lay hold on it, and lift it out? How much then is a man better than a _____?"

265. The lions left Daniel alone, thanks to God's angel, but they did get to break the bones of __ __ __?

266. What kind of bird, in the Bible, is said to sit on eggs that don't hatch?
    A. the partridge
    B. the dove

C. the red hen
D. the kiwi

267. Besides the dove, Noah sent a _____ out of the ark.

268. In Matthew, Jesus made his triumphal entry into Jerusalem, as had been predicted in the book of Zechariah (9:9), riding on the colt of what animal?

269. "It is easier for a _____ to go through the eye of a needle, than for a rich man to enter into the kingdom of God."

270. Who named the animals that God made? Was it—
    A. God
    B. Adam
    C. the prophets
    D. different men

16. *Hidden Books*

If you look carefully at these sentences, ignoring punctuation, you'll be able to ferret out the names of twenty books of the Bible—one to a sentence.

271. HE PLAYS BANJO BADLY, BUT SINGS WELL.

272. TIPS, ALMS, INHERITANCES: ALL ARE TAX-ABLE.

273. MAN NAMED EUGENE. SISTER NAMED JU-DITH. NO FURTHER INFO.

274. I'M AT THE WINDOW LOOKING OUT ONTO THE LAWN.

275. I AM A FRANCOPHILE, MONSIEUR. ET VOUS?

276. NUR EINMAL? ACH! ICH BIN ENTTÄUSCHT!

277. HE NEVER WENT OUT WITHOUT TAKING A WALKING STICK.

278. AFTER VISITING JORDAN, I ELECTED TO GO HOME.

279. YES, A MOST INTERESTING BOOK, I THOUGHT.

280. WEATHER FORECAST: STORM. ARK NEEDS REPAIRS. PLEASE ADVISE.

281. ISN'T IT USELESS TO PROTEST TO THEM?

282. THE OLDEST HERITAGE ISN'T NECESSARILY THE BEST.

283. A BUSHEL OF APPLES, ALL RIPE: TERRIFIC!

284. IS JAM ESSENTIAL TO A PEANUT BUTTER SANDWICH?

285. THOSE AREN'T THE ONES I ASKED FOR.

286. A COMIC, A HOLLYWOOD AGENT, AND A PRODUCER HAD LUNCH.

287. ANNA, HUMBLE ANNA, DEAR SWEET ANNA!

288. "THIS TIME THE BREW SHOULD HAVE ITS EFFECT," SAID THE WITCH.

289. HE ALMOST LOST HIS FEZ, RACING UP THE STEPS.

290. THAT'S THE "MONA LISA," I—AH—THINK. OR IS IT "GUERNICA"?

17. Which Comes First?

291. Eve's eating the Forbidden Fruit, or Adam's?

292. Cain or Abel? (Who was older?)

293. The Tower of Babel or The Flood?

294. Jacob or Esau? (Which twin was born first?)

295. The plague of lice or the plague of frogs?

296. Locusts or darkness?

297. "Thou shalt not kill" or "Thou shalt not steal"?

298. "Thou shalt not commit adultery" or "Thou shalt not bear false witness against thy neighbour"?

299. Ahab or Omri as king of Israel?

300. Uzziah (also known as Azaria) or Amaziah?

301. Daniel in the lions' den or Jonah in the great fish's stomach? (Which story appears first in the Bible?)

302. The commandment to love God or the commandment to love thy neighbor as thyself, as quoted by Jesus?

303. Leviticus or Exodus? (Which book comes first?)

304. Psalms or Proverbs? (Which book comes first?)

305. Thessalonians or Colossians? (Which book comes first?)

18. Which King...?

The Bible is packed with kings doing good and evil. Remembering who did what isn't always easy. For instance...

306. Which king ordered slain all the children in and around Bethlehem age two and under?

307. Which king (the king of which city?) joined his people in repenting by fasting, laying down his robe, covering himself with sackcloth, and sitting in ashes?

308. Which king went in disguise to ask a medium to summon up the sprit of Samuel?

309. Which king was made to eat grass like an ox?

310. Which king chided his servants for having brought him David, who appeared to be mad?

311. Which king had an iron bed that was nine cubits long and four cubits broad?

312. Which king burned a scroll dictated by the prophet Jeremiah, and as punishment from God had the throne taken away from his family line?

313. Which king was influenced by his wives to take up idolatry, angering the Lord?

314. Which king "did more to provoke the Lord God of Israel to anger than all the kings of Israel that were before him"?

315. Which king had the records of his reign read to him when he couldn't sleep?

Now match the king with the brief words that fit.

316. Followed Solomon to the throne.   Ahasuerus

317. Jesus called him "that fox."   David

318. God called him "a man after mine own heart."   Ahab

319. A Gentile, he made Esther his queen.   Herod

320. He went into battle wearing a disguise.   Rehoboam

19. Words of God

A quiz on the direct words of God, as quoted in the Bible. Some are particularly tough.

321. Complete: "Come now, and let us _____ _____."

322. What did God ask Ezekiel about the dry bones in the valley?

323. God promised a prophet, "There shall yet old men and old women dwell in the streets of Jerusalem, and every man with his staff in his hand for very age. And the streets of the city shall be full of boys and girls playing in the streets thereof." Which prophet?

324. God promised, through the prophet Joel, that "your sons and your daughters shall prophesy, your old men shall dream dreams, your young men shall _____ _____."

325. Did God ever say that Jesus was his beloved Son?

In the next five, read the quote and pick the person to whom God said it.

326. "Get thee out of thy country, and from thy kindred, and from thy father's house, unto a land that I will shew thee."
    A. Abram
    B. Moses
    C. Aaron
    D. Naomi

327. "I Am That I Am...Thus shalt thou say unto the children of Israel, I Am hath sent me unto you."
    A. Jesus
    B. Luke
    C. Moses
    D. Noah

328. "Be strong and of a good courage."
    A. Joshua
    B. Job
    C. Daniel
    D. David

329. "Hast thou an arm like God? or canst thou thunder with a voice like him?"
    A. Joshua
    B. Ezekiel
    C. Daniel
    D. Job

330. "Because thou hast done this, thou art cursed...."
    A. Cain
    B. the serpent
    C. Eve
    D. Adam

20. Hidden Words—Places

331-365. Find the names of thirty-five Biblical places in this letter grid.

S	H	E	B	R	O	N	E	A	T	Y	R	A	V	L	A	C
A	L	D	E	S	O	E	B	E	I	H	A	B	T	G	S	A
L	A	N	T	E	L	R	A	L	T	N	E	R	P	I	U	R
A	G	U	H	I	S	T	L	N	E	B	O	H	Y	S	C	M
M	L	H	L	C	G	U	Q	U	H	C	M	D	G	J	S	E
I	I	A	E	A	F	A	R	A	A	T	N	L	E	F	A	L
S	G	M	H	N	F	G	B	P	F	L	E	R	L	C	M	C
P	A	H	E	A	S	R	E	O	Y	N	I	R	R	O	A	D
U	L	A	M	A	P	R	M	T	U	C	Y	E	A	J	D	M
N	A	I	V	N	N	A	E	O	H	E	I	A	K	Z	K	Z
N	T	R	B	A	H	G	L	O	A	S	N	P	M	F	A	Y
O	I	O	U	C	D	A	A	F	N	B	E	T	H	E	L	N
R	A	M	E	I	P	S	S	Z	J	J	A	M	X	N	A	Y
H	U	I	W	P	S	N	U	K	A	L	P	M	A	D	O	D
P	R	N	O	O	P	H	R	Y	G	I	A	I	R	N	R	B
I	I	J	S	L	O	B	E	R	E	A	N	O	M	C	E	F
Z	I	O	N	K	I	R	J	A	T	H	J	E	A	R	I	M

50

21. One-Word Answers—Old Testament

Fill in the blanks—one word at a time.

366. The world's first clothes, made by God for Adam and Eve, were of _____.

367. Cherubim were placed at the _____ of the garden of Eden.

368. Which of the Lord's hands did the Israelites credit with saving them from the Egyptians? The _____ hand.

369. During the Exodus, Joshua fought Amalek after Moses produced _____.

370. The Lord ordered the children of Israel to forever remind themselves of his commandments by wearing fringes with a ribband coloured _____.

371. "A bastard shall not enter into the congregation of the Lord: even to his _____ generation shall he not enter into the congregation of the Lord."

372. Who's next in this line: Aphiah, Bechorath, Zeror, Abiel, Kish, _____.

373. David and Goliath both wore helmets of _____.

374. Absalom killed his brother Amnon for raping _____.

375. When God came to Solomon in a dream, the king asked not for riches or honor or long life, but for the wisdom to be a good _____.

376. When the people begged Rehoboam to lighten their burden, he heard advice from old and young. He listened to the _____.

377. The _____ licked the blood of King Ahab, as was predicted by Elijah.

378. Children mocked Elisha the prophet on the road to Bethel, noting that he was _____.

379. In answer, Elisha cursed the children and they were attacked by two _____.

380. Was Job rich or poor? He was _____.

381. "Ecclesiastes; Or, the _____."

382. From the Song of Solomon: "His _____ hand is under my head, and his _____ hand doth embrace me."

383. Jeremiah tried to get them to drink wine. They were tentdwellers. They were the _____.

384. "Prepare to meet thy God, O _____."

385. According to Micah, the Lord requires man to walk _____ with him.

22. Occupations

Here are three matching quizzes that ask you to tell how different Biblical characters made their livings. First, five fairly easy ones.

386. Joseph, husband of Mary   tiller of the ground

387. Simon, called Peter   shepherd

388. Cain   fisherman

389. David   hunter

390. Esau   carpenter

Next, five that are a little tougher to place.

391. Paul   cupbearer to the
                             king

392. Abel   tentmaker

393. Amos   keeper of sheep

394. Nehemiah   beggar

395. Lazarus   herdman

Finally, five for the experts.

396. Rahab   midwife

397. Shebna   harlot

398. Gehazi   handmaid to Sarai

399. Hagar   scribe

400. Shiphrah   servant

23. How Did They Die?

On the left, descriptions of how they died; on the right, who they were. Match.

401. Hanged on the very gallows he had prepared for Mordecai.

Stephen

402. Stoned to death, at the Lord's bidding.

Herod

403. Thrown from a window.

Haman

404. Hanged himself (according to Matthew).

Saul

405. "Fell down, and gave up the ghost" upon being confronted with the sin of withholding money from the church and lying about it.

Eli

406. Stoned to death for preaching that Jesus was the saviour. Samson

407. Struck down by the angel of the Lord, and eaten of worms. Jezebel

408. Fell backward off his seat upon hearing that God's ark had been taken by the Philistines; broke his neck and died. Judas Iscariot

409. Committed suicide with a sword as the Philistines closed in, as told in 1 Samuel. Ananias

410. Pulled down pillars of Philistine meeting hall, killing himself and crowd. The man who gathered sticks on the sabbath

And another ten who died.

411. Hanged, in accordance with the dream interpreted by Joseph.

Balaam

412. Stricken by the plague.

The Pharoah's chief baker

413. Killed in battle by a sword.

Eutychus

414. Killed by Ehud's dagger.

Agag the king of the Amalekites

415. Jael hammered a nail into his temples as he slept.

Absalom

416. Fell asleep and tumbled from the window of a third loft.

Nadab and Abihus, the bad sons of Aaron

417. Cut into pieces by Samuel at Gilgal.

The ten members of the search party who recommended abandoning the quest for the Promised Land

418. Died at the hand of God.

Eglon, king of Moab

419. Shot through the heart by three darts from Joab, as he hung by his head from an oak tree; ten young men completed the killing.

Uzzah, the man who touched the ark

420. Burned.

Sisera, the Canaanite captain

24. Opening Words

Can you identify the Bible book just by reading its opening words? Match the books to the beginnings.

421. "These be the words which Moses spake unto all Israel...."   Genesis

422. "Now these are the names of the children of Israel...."   Leviticus

423. "In the beginning God created the heaven and the earth."   Exodus

424. "And the Lord spake unto Moses in the wilderness of Sinai...."   Deuteronomy

425. "And the Lord called unto Moses, and spake unto him out of the tabernacle of the congregation...."   Numbers

426. "Now it came to pass, in the days when the judges ruled, that there was a famine in the land."　　1 Kings

427. "Now it came to pass, in the days of Ahasuerus...."　　1 Chronicles

428. "Now king David was old and stricken with years; and they covered him with clothes, but he gat no heat."　　Psalms

429. "Blessed is the man that walketh not in the counsel of the ungodly...."　　Esther

430. "Adam, Sheth, Enosh...."　　Ruth

431. "In the beginning was the Word and the Word was with God, and the Word was God."　　Matthew

432. "The beginning of the gospel of Jesus Christ, the Son of God."　　Mark

433. "The former treatise have I made, O Theophilus...."　　Luke

434. "The book of the generation of Jesus Christ, the son of David, the son of Abraham."　　John

435. "Forasmuch as many have taken in hand to set forth in order a declaration...."　　Acts

25. Last Words

Now match five more books to their *last* words.

436. "So Joseph died, being an hundred and ten years old: and they embalmed him, and he was put in a coffin in Egypt."

Psalms

437. "And there are also many other things which Jesus did, the which, if they should be written every one, I suppose that even the world itself could not contain the books that should be written."

Genesis

438. "For God shall bring every work into judgment, with every secret thing, whether it be good, or whether it be evil."

Ecclesiastes

439. "Let every thing that hath breath praise the Lord. Praise ye the Lord."

Song of Solomon

62

440. "Make haste, my beloved, and be   John
thou like to a roe, or to a young
hart, upon the mountains of
spices."

26. Food and Drink

From the Forbidden Fruit in Eden to The Last Supper, things to eat and drink pop up here and there in the Bible. See how well you remember.

441. The men Moses sent to investigate the land of Canaan returned to report that, as promised (Exodus 3:17), "it floweth with _____ and _____."

442. Which of the following do we know Moses' followers found in Canaan?
    A. grapes
    B. pomegranates
    C. figs
    D. oranges
    E. citrons

443. According to Paul's advice, Timothy should stop drinking water and "use a little wine." Why?

444. When three visitors came to Abraham at Mamre, to tell him that Sarah would bear him a child, Abraham was properly hospitable. After he invited them into his tent, what did he give them to eat and drink?
    A. lamb and wine
    B. lamb, milk, and cakes
    C. cakes, dressed calf, butter, and milk
    D. kid, sweet cakes, and frozen milk

445. Of their twins, Rebekah preferred Jacob, but Isaac favored Esau, "because he did eat of his _____."

446. It wasn't just pottage that Jacob gave Esau after they reached an agreement over the birthright; he also served him _____.
    A. bread
    B. grapes and figs
    C. meat
    D. milk

447. What did Joseph's brothers eat after they threw him into the pit?

448. The Lord commanded the Israelites to make the Passover sacrifice and feast on roast lamb, unleavened bread, and _____ _____.

449. This Old Testament edible was described as being "a small round thing, as small as the hoar frost on the ground." What was it?

450. What food did God send the Israelites in such great abundance that they ate themselves sick?

451. Whom did the Lord command to feed Elijah, and what was he fed?

452. According to the Book of Isaiah, Immanuel would eat this "that he may know to refuse the evil, and choose the good." What?

453. What did the Lord make Ezekiel eat that isn't normally considered food?
    A. a soldier's boot
    B. leaves of a tree
    C. a roll of a book
    D. dry bones

454. What lesson of nutrition did Daniel give Melzar?

455. When John the Baptist first went "preaching in the wilderness of Judaea, he ate"—
    A. bread and butter
    B. manna and milk
    C. locusts and wild honey
    D. nothing at all

456. After the resurrection, Jesus asked the apostles, "Have ye here any meat?" They gave him "a piece of _____ _____ and of an _____," which he ate.

457. When the Israelites were living on a diet of manna in the wilderness, they longingly dreamed of the foods they had eaten in Egypt. Tell which of these was *not* on their list: fish, cucumbers, melons, apples, leeks, onions, garlick.

458. What, according to Solomon, "biteth like a serpent, and stingeth like an adder"?

459. According to 1 Kings, Solomon's provision for one day included "thirty measures of _____, and three score measures of _____."

460. In Leviticus, the Lord told Moses: "With all thine offerings thou shalt offer _____."
    A. bread
    B. salt
    C. fruit
    D. lamb

461. Sisera, the captain of Jabin's army, asked Jael, wife of Heber the Kenite, "Give me, I pray thee, a little water to drink; for I am thirsty." Jael gave him no water; instead she gave him—
    A. vinegar
    B. milk
    C. wine
    D. nothing at all

462. In the Book of Nahum, what was it that would fall into the mouth of the eater, if only the tree should be shaken? Was it—
    A. figs
    B. dates
    C. oranges
    D. apples

463. What kind of nuts did Aaron's rod yield, when it had blossomed?
    A. walnuts
    B. hickory nuts
    C. peanuts
    D. almonds

464. The Gibeonites were spared thanks to old clothes, old shoes, and what kind of bread?

465. Paul wrote to the Colossians: "Let your speech be always with grace, seasoned with _____, that ye may know how ye ought to answer every man."
    A. coriander
    B. rare seeds
    C. hot pepper
    D. salt

27. More Who's Who

Another batch of capsule identifications. These are tougher than the first, but if you've read the stories well you should know who's who. First initials and number of letters in each name help make things a little easier.

466. He was the prophet who was put in the stocks as punishment from Chief Governor Pashur: J _ _ _ _ _ _ _.

467. His father was Amaziah, king of Judah, his mother Jecholiah (Jecoliah) of Jerusalem; he became king of Judah at 16: A _ _ _ _ _ _.

468. He alone among the sons of Jerubbaal escaped death at the hand of Abimelech, by hiding: J _ _ _ _ _.

469. He told David that Saul was out to kill him; then he persuaded Saul to let David live—for a while: J _ _ _ _ _ _ _.

470. He brought back to life the son of the widow in whose house he was staying: E _ _ _ _ _.

471. He purified the waters of Jericho with salt and the power of the Lord: E _ _ _ _ _ _ _.

472. When he saw the infant Jesus at the temple in Jerusalem, he lifted him in his arms and blessed him, saying, "Lord, now lettest thou thy servant depart in peace, according to thy word; For mine eyes have seen thy salvation...": S _ _ _ _ _.

473. Of him it was said: "Foxes have holes, and birds of the air have nests; but _ _ _ _ _ _ _ hath not where to lay his head": J _ _ _ _.

474. He climbed up into a sycamore tree, the better to see Jesus: Z _ _ _ _ _ _ _ _.

475. He was the high priest's servant who lost an ear at Gethsemane: M _ _ _ _ _ _.

476. He begged Pilate for the body of Jesus, and entombed him: J _ _ _ _ _ (of Arimathaea).

477. Paul and Barnabas argued over him, leading to their split: J _ _ _ M _ _ _.

478. When they saw that Canaan was populated by men stronger than they, ten spies suggested returning to Egypt; these two proposed marching on, saying, "The Lord is with us: fear them not": C _ _ _ _ and J _ _ _ _ _.

479. He replaced his father, Aaron, in a ceremony at Mount Hor: E _ _ _ _ _ _.

480. He disobeyed the Lord and kept some of the spoils of Jericho for himself, causing divine punishment in the form of a defeat at the hands of the men of Ai: A _ _ _ _.

481. He was left-handed, and he made a two-edged dagger that was a cubit in length: E _ _ _.

482. He said of Joseph, "Let us not kill him," but he proposed throwing Joseph into a pit: R _ _ _ _ _.

483. He "walked with God after he begat Methuselah": E _ _ _ _.

484. He was the Egyptian captain who bought Joseph from the Midianites: P _ _ _ _ _ _ _.

485. "Who, when he was reviled, reviled not again ...": J _ _ _ _.

28. Numbers

You needn't be a math whiz to pass this test, but you have to remember people's ages, amounts of money, and other numbers from the Scriptures.

486. Methuselah lived _____ years.

487. Noah's ark was thirty cubits high, fifty cubits wide, and _____ cubits long.

488. King Saul was annoyed to hear the popular expression of the day, "Saul hath slain his thousands, and David his _____."

489. How many men were sent to fetch Elijah?

490. When Moses died, he was—
      A. one hundred twenty years old

B. one hundred sixty years old
C. four hundred forty nine years old
D. threescore and ten years old

491. Jonah was in the belly of the great fish _____ days and _____ nights.

492. For how many days was Saul without sight in Damascus?

493. How many times did Jesus say Peter should forgive his brother's sinning against him?

494. Jesus sent _____ disciples, two by two, into every place he was to go.

495. In the parable of the ten virgins, how many were wise and how many foolish?

496. The false witnesses before the chief priests and elders and council of the Jews testified that Jesus declared he could destroy the temple and rebuild it himself in _____ days.

497. How old was David when he became king of Israel?

498. What were the odds when the priests of Baal and Elijah met to decide the true God?
    A. ten to one
    B. one hundred to one
    C. four hundred fifty to one
    D. one thousand to one

499. When Elisha revived the dead son of the rich woman in Shunem, the boy sneezed. How many sneezes?

500. To whom does this census refer: "The whole congregation together was forty and two thousand three hundred and threescore. Beside their servants and their maids, of whom there were seven thousand three hundred thirty and seven: and there were among them two hundred singing men and singing women. Their horses were seven hundred thirty and six; their mules, two hundred forty and five; Their camels, four hundred thirty and five; their asses, six thousand seven hundred and twenty."

501. Joseph's burial plot became his children's inheritance; it had been bought by Jacob for _____ pieces of silver.
    A. one hundred
    B. one thousand
    C. thirty
    D. forty

502. When Jesus changed water into wine, there were _____ waterpots of stone.

503. What did Jacob promise to give to God? (What fraction of his bounty?)

504. After the Israelites escaped from Egypt, they came to Moriah and found the water bitter. Then they pushed on to Elim, where they found _____ wells of water and _____ palm trees.

505. When Moses complained that he was not strong enough to lead the Exodus alone, the Lord appointed a council of elders to share the burden. How many of them?

506. How many times did Samuel go to Eli, thinking he had heard him call?

74

507. The Levites were to be given forty-eight cities in the Promised Land, of which _____ were to be cities of refuge for manslayers.
    A. four
    B. five
    C. six
    D. twelve

508. How many were slaughtered when the men of Bethshemesh looked into the ark of the Lord?

509. How old was Joseph when he received the coat of many colours?

510. How many pairs of each clean beast did Noah take aboard the ark?

511. How many years did Jacob serve Laban before he earned the right to marry Laban's daughter, Rachel?

512. The rains lasted forty days and forty nights, but how long was it until the waters finally abated?
    A. forty days and forty nights more
    B. one year
    C. a day
    D. one hundred fifty days

513. How many times did Noah send the dove from the ark?

514. At first the Lord said he would spare Sodom if fifty righteous persons could be found there, but Abraham was able to argue him down to _____.

515. How many psalms are there in the Old Testament?

516. "The days of our years," meaning our lifespan, are numbered at...?

517. The city of twelve gates was to be about _____ measures round.

518. How long did Mary, mother-to-be of Jesus, live with Elizabeth, mother-to-be of John the Baptist?
    A. about three months
    B. about a week
    C. one day and one night
    D. thirty-six hours

519. How long was the boy Jesus lost from his parents in Jerusalem?

520. On his way to Jerusalem, Jesus met _____ lepers. Of these, he cured _____. Of them, only _____ returned to thank him.

29. The Number Forty

The number forty keeps popping up all over the Bible. In fact, every blank in this quiz can be properly filled in with "forty"... except two. Which?

521. During the Great Flood it rained for _____ days and _____ nights.

522. Moses and the Jews wandered in the desert for _____ years before reaching the Promised Land.

523. Moses himself spent _____ years in the desert before the Exodus.

524. Moses fasted on Mount Sinai for _____ days and _____ nights.

525. Moses sent a search party of twelve—one for each tribe—to scout the land of Canaan. "They returned from searching of the land after _____ days."

526. Jesus fasted for _____ days in the wilderness, before starting his teaching.

527. Elijah went without eating for _____ days and _____ nights.

528. When Jonah finally went to Nineveh, he preached to the people, saying that the city would be overthrown in _____ days.

529. Judas Iscariot betrayed his master for _____ pieces of silver.

530. Moses was _____ years old when he smote the Egyptian.

531. How long was David king? _____ years.

532. And Solomon was king for _____ years.

533. For how many days did Jesus show himself before he ascended to heaven? For _____ days.

534. Jehoash was _____ years old when he began to reign over Israel.

535. More than _____ Jews vowed to fast until they had killed Paul in Jerusalem.

30. The Miracles of Jesus

A brief, ten-question quiz on details of some of the miraculous deeds of Jesus, as reported by the Four Evangelists.

536. What and where was Jesus' first miracle?

537. Where did Jesus get the loaves and fishes to feed the multitude, according to John?

538. How was Jesus addressed by the two blind men he cured?
   A. "Sire"
   B. "O Lord"
   C. "Thou son of David"
   D. "Mr. Messiah"

539. Was it the son or the daughter of Jairus, the ruler of the synagogue, that Jesus raised from the dead?

540. To whom did Jesus command, "Young man, I say unto thee, Arise," and where did this miracle take place?

541. Jesus said, "I have not found so great faith, no, not in Israel." Then he healed...?

542. When Jesus told Simon to let his net into the lake, the fisherman snared an abundance of fish. What two unfortunate events followed?

543. At what time did Jesus heal the son of "a certain nobleman" of Capernaum?
    A. at the seventh hour
    B. at the twelfth hour
    C. at eventide
    D. at noon plus a half

544. Of what did Jesus cure Simon's wife's mother at Capernaum?
    A. leprosy
    B. fever
    C. crippled leg
    D. crippled arms

545. The Jews were angered by the curing of the invalid at Bethesda because...?

31. Words of Jesus

How well do you know what Jesus said, to whom he said it, and under what circumstances? Start your test by trying to complete these quotations.

546. Jesus commanded the disciples: "Go ye therefore, and teach all nations, baptizing them...."

547. Jesus said the temple should be a house of prayer "but ye have made it a _____ of _____."

548. "Judge not...."

549. "Give not that which is holy unto the dogs...."

550. "Ask, and it shall be given you...."

551. "Blessed are the pure in heart...."

552. "And if thy right eye offend thee...."

553. "I am the root and the offspring of _____."

554. "Among those that are born of women, there is not a greater prophet than...."

555. As Jesus was led to Calvary, he said to the crying women: "Daughters of Jerusalem...."

Now tell to whom Jesus was speaking when he said these lines.

556. "Why persecutest thou me?"

557. "Get thee behind me, Satan."

558. "Blessed be ye poor: for yours is the kingdom of God."

559. "It is written, Man shall not live by bread alone, but by every word that proceedeth out of the mouth of God."

560. "O thou of little faith, wherefore didst thou doubt?"

561. "For God so loved the world, that he gave his only begotten Son, that whosoever believeth in him should not perish, but have everlasting life."

562. "Thou shalt love the Lord thy God with all thy heart, and with all thy soul, and with all thy mind."

563. "Take nothing for your journey, neither staves, nor scrip, neither bread, neither money; neither have two coats apiece."

564. "Fear not: believe only, and she shall be made whole."

565. "Follow me, and I will make you fishers of men."

And now, a mixture of twenty final questions on the words of Jesus.

566. Jesus told a parable about a wise man who built his house on rock and a foolish man who built his house
_____ _____.

567. Jesus said that a divided kingdom cannot stand, and a divided house cannot stand. But this was just leading up to his saying—what?

568. What did Jesus answer when the Jews asked him if he had seen Abraham?
   A. "I have, and he hath seen me as well."
   B. "Before Abraham was, I am."
   C. "Father Abraham spake unto me but I did not see him bodily."
   D. "Over and over, and over once again."

569. What does Jesus say is the fate of "all things that offend, and them which do iniquity"?

570. When Jesus asked, "Who touched my clothes?" who, in fact, had touched them? And what happened?

571. "Be of good cheer; it is I: be not afraid." Under what circumstances did Jesus say this?

572. What will happen, according to Jesus, "if the blind lead the blind"?

573. When Jesus went to the synagogue at Nazareth, he read from the book of Isaiah and then told the congregation: "This day is the scripture. . . ."

574. Upon seeing Matthew, or Levi, Jesus said two words to him. What words?
    A. "Hail, Matthew!"
    B. "Hail, Levi!"
    C. "Follow me."
    D. "God bless."

575. How did Jesus say to give alms?
    A. generously
    B. unendingly
    C. secretly
    D. compassionately

576. "He was a murderer from the beginning, and abode not in the truth, because there is no truth in him." Of whom was Jesus speaking?

577. In the Book of Matthew, Jesus follows The Lord's Prayer by saying, "For if ye forgive men their trespasses, your heavenly Father will also forgive you." True or false?

578. According to Jesus, for what does the good shepherd give his life?

579. Complete: "Every one that exalteth himself shall be abased; and he that humbleth himself _____ _____ _____."

580. When Jesus said, "He that is without sin among you, let him first cast a stone at her," what sinner was he defending?

581. "It is more blessed to give than to receive." Who quoted Jesus as saying that?

582. What parable did Jesus tell to suggest that God forgives those who forgive their debtors?

583. Jesus said that God can't know what you need until you pray for it. True or false?

584. The Good Samaritan, in the parable told by Jesus, helped—
   A. a man who had been robbed
   B. a man who had fallen ill
   C. a man who had tried to kill himself
   D. a woman whose husband had beaten her

585. Did Jesus say, "Father, forgive them; for they know not what they do" before or after he was nailed to the cross?

32. Multiple Choice—Old Testament

586. When Nebuchadnezzar saw that Shadrach, Meshach, and Abednego were unharmed by a blazing fire, he decreed that thenceforth anyone who spoke ill of their God would be—
    A. cast into a burning fiery furnace
    B. ostracized
    C. punished by slaying of the first-born in his family
    D. cut in pieces, and their houses shall be made a dunghill

587. Who did the Lord tell Ezekiel were worthy of being saved if they were in the doomed land?
    A. Job and his three friends
    B. Solomon, his mother, and all his descendants
    C. Noah, Daniel, and Job (and none of their children)
    D. Abraham, Isaac, and Jacob

588. When Joseph interpreted the Pharoah's dream, he was rewarded with, among other things—
    A. a ring
    B. a bracelet of pure gold
    C. an hundred camels and an hundred asses
    D. a gilded chariot

589. What will happen to a man "that diggeth a pit," according to Ecclesiastes? He'll—
    A. fall into it
    B. find that he has dug in vain
    C. be scorned by his brethren
    D. enter into the kingdom of God

590. "He was oppressed, and he was afflicted," says the Book of Isaiah, "yet...."
    A. "...he knew not pain."
    B. "...he knew not how to overcome."
    C. "...he opened not his mouth."
    D. "...he praised the Lord with his tongue and in his heart."

591. When the priests of Baal prayed for a sign, nothing happened. Elijah, the prophet of the Lord—
    A. cried
    B. looked the other way
    C. cried out, "I fear that my Lord, too, shall keep his silence!"
    D. made fun of the priests

592. Jehu drove his chariot—
    A. carefully
    B. slowly
    C. drunkenly
    D. furiously

593. The Lord smote 185,000 Assyrians under King
Sennacherib, much to the relief of—
A. Sharezer
B. Hezekiah
C. David
D. Ahaz

594. The elders of Israel disapproved of Samuel's sons, Joel
and Abiah, because—
A. they worshiped golden idols
B. they were greedy and took bribes
C. they spoke in a strange and perplexing manner
D. they lusted after the Philistine women

595. What was unusual about the manner of construction of
Solomon's temple?
A. it was built entirely by Egyptian slaves
B. it was built entirely of cedar wood, with no
stone at all
C. it was at least partially prefabricated with stone
precut off-site
D. it was built on a twenty-four-hour-a-day basis,
with crews laboring through the nights for a
month

596. The harlot who sheltered the two Israelites from the
king of Jericho asked in return that they—
A. pay her forty shekels of silver
B. say a prayer for her every day for a year
C. refrain from attacking Jericho
D. assure her and her family of protection during
the siege of Jericho

597. Who told Gideon to save Israel from the Midianites?
A. an angel
B. two angels

C. the Lord

D. Deborah

598. Only two of the original party of Israelites survived the trip through the wilderness. They were—
    A. Moses and Aaron
    B. Miriam and Aaron
    C. Joshua and Caleb
    D. Balaam and Balak

599. To whom did the Old Testament Joseph say, "I am Joseph; doth my father yet live?"
    A. his mother
    B. his brothers
    C. the Pharaoh
    D. Rebekah

600. In the first plague, the Lord turned a body of water to blood. Was it—
    A. the Dead Sea
    B. the ocean
    C. the river
    D. the Pharaoh's private swimming pool

601. When Abram took Hagar as a wife, Sarai—
    A. was displeased, for it was not God's will
    B. was jealous, for she hated Hagar
    C. was responsible, for she had suggested it
    D. did not know, for she was in another land

602. Who were Shem, Ham, and Japheth?
    A. the wise men
    B. sons of Noah
    C. sons of Adam
    D. kings of Judah

603. David escaped from Achish the king of Gath by—
    A. disguising himself as a woman
    B. riding away on an ass at night
    C. feigning madness
    D. asking the Lord to make Achish blind and deaf

604. The Lord answered Job—
    A. "in a foreign tongue"
    B. "out of the whirlwind"
    C. "with a fierce anger"
    D. "in a tone he had not before heard"

605. The Book of Lamentations was written by—
    A. Ezekiel
    B. Jeremiah
    C. Amos
    D. Obadiah

33. Women in the Bible

A chapter on the Bible's wives, mothers, queens, and assorted other women.

606. Miriam and Aaron criticized Moses for marrying a woman who was—
    A. Egyptian
    B. Roman
    C. Greek
    D. Ethiopian

607. She was wife of King Ahab. God promised that at her death she would be devoured by dogs. Who was she?

608. What was the Lord's punishment for Miriam, who spoke against Moses?
    A. baldness
    B. leprosy
    C. boils and sores
    D. infertility

609. She died in childbirth, calling her son Benoni. But his father named him Benjamin. Who was she?

610. Unnamed, she tried to seduce Joseph, son of Jacob. When he refused her advances, she accused him of attacking her and had him thrown in prison. Identify her.

611. She hid two Israelite spies on the roof of her house in Jericho, saving them from the king.

612. Jephthah made a vow to the Lord that resulted in his having to slay his daughter, his only child. But how long did he wait before carrying out the vow? Was it—
    A. two months
    B. two years
    C. twenty years
    D. unstated

613. What did Pilate's wife say to her husband about the trial of Jesus?

614. What did the women bring to the sepulcher where Jesus had been buried?

615. The angel of the Lord appeared to her and told her that she would bear a son who would deliver Israel from the Philistines.

616. Ruth's mother-in-law was Naomi, but who was her father-in-law? Was it—
    A. Abraham
    B. Isaac
    C. Elimelech
    D. David

617. She said: "My soul doth magnify the Lord. And my spirit hath rejoiced in God my Saviour. For he hath regarded the low state of his handmaiden: for, behold, from henceforth all generations shall call me blessed." Who was she?

618. Barren Hannah was praying to the Lord that he give her a child. Eli the priest observed her moving lips, which issued forth no sound, and concluded that she was _____.

619. How did Michal, David's wife, fool the king's messengers and help David to escape?

620. She came from afar to witness for herself the wisdom of Solomon, and ended by giving him spices and gold.
    A. Jezebel
    B. the queen of Sheba
    C. the queen of Jordan
    D. an unnamed "regal lady"

621. She was at the temple when Joseph and Mary brought Jesus to be presented to the Lord with a sacrifice.

622. She asked for John the Baptist's head, and got it.

623. "The king Ahasuerus commanded" her "to be brought in before him, but she came not." Who was she?

624. According to her, "it is not for kings to drink wine, nor for princes strong drink." Was she—
    A. the mother of king Lemuel
    B. the daughter of king Lemuel
    C. the sister of king Lemuel
    D. Hagar

625. They "committed whoredoms in Egypt," said the Lord to Ezekiel. Name them and tell their relationship.

34. Other Names

Some Biblical men and women were known, at different times and in different places, by names other than the ones we know best. Given four choices, see if you can pick the right alias.

626. Abraham—
    A. Abram
    B. Bram
    C. Aaron
    D. Jephtha-loka

627. Sarah—
    A. Rebeccah
    B. Sararan
    C. Sarai
    D. Soroh

628. The apostle Paul—
    A. Peter
    B. Chad
    C. Saul
    D. Oded

629. Queen Esther—
    A. Essie
    B. Eliz
    C. Ethel
    D. Hadassah

630. Daniel—
    A. Belteshazzar
    B. Shadrach
    C. Meshach
    D. Nehemiah

35. Biblical Brothers

Match brother to brother.

631. The apostle Peter   Seth

632. The apostle James   Benjamin

633. Nadab   John

634. Joseph, son of Jacob   Andrew

635. Cain   Abihu

36. Yes or No?

One word is all the answer that's needed here. Either "yes" or "no" will do the trick. The questions are all taken from the New Testament.

636. Did the resurrected Jesus appear first to Mary Magdalene?

637. Did Mary ever witness a miracle performed by her son, Jesus?

638. Jesus was bitten by a viper but "he shook off the beast into the fire, and felt no harm." Right?

639. Does the word "Amen" appear at the conclusion of The Lord's Prayer as it is read in the book of Matthew?

640. When John the Baptist was born, did his mother say his name was to be John because it had been ordained by an angel?

641. Did three wise men from the east come to visit Jesus, according to Matthew?

642. Did Jesus say that for a man just to look at a woman with lustful intent is to commit adultery in his heart?

643. Can a bad tree give good fruit, according to Jesus?

644. After Jesus exorcised the demons from the man on the other side of the sea, in the country of the Gadarenes, did he tell the man to keep quiet about the healing?

645. Is The Lord's Prayer given twice in the Bible?

646. When Jesus was asked which is the greatest commandment of all, he answered, "Thou shalt love thy neighbor as thyself." Right?

647. According to Matthew, did Judas Iscariot refuse to return the bribe he had received for betraying Jesus, asking "Hath the Lord himself so ordained?"

648. After the crucifixion, one of the Roman soldiers pierced Jesus in the side with a spear. Did blood flow?

649. Was the jailer who put Paul and Silas in the stocks eventually baptized?

650. When Barnabas and Saul preached among the Gentiles, were they careful never to go inside the synagogues of the Jews?

37. One-Word Answers—New Testament

651. "For the law was given by Moses, but grace and _____ came by Jesus Christ."

652. When Jesus was baptized, the Spirit of God came down in the shape of a _____.

653. "For what is a man profited, if he shall gain the whole world, and lose his own _____?"

654. Jesus cured the blind man with clay made from dirt on the ground and _____.

655. What day was it that Jesus healed the blind man?

656. Jesus said: "The Son of man cometh at an hour when ye _____ not."

657. Bartimaeus' affliction, cured by Jesus at the roadside as he went out of Jericho: _____.

658. Jesus caused a _____ tree to wither, and then told his disciples, "And all things whatsoever ye shall ask in prayer, believing, ye shall receive."

659. The Book of Matthew contains the parable of the marriage feast, in which a king invites people to the wedding of his _____.

660. When Jesus was asked if it was proper to pay tribute to Caesar, before he answered he asked to be brought a _____.

661. "The spirit indeed is willing, but the flesh is weak," said Jesus, when he found the disciples _____.

662. Simon Peter, according to John, was the apostle who cut off the right _____ of the high priest's servant, come to arrest Jesus.

663. Mark and Luke say Barabbas was a murderer, but John says he was a _____.

664. _____ others were crucified on the hill with Jesus.

665. When Mary Magdalene saw the resurrected Jesus, she thought he was the _____.

666. Ananias sold _____ to get money for the apostles.

667. When Paul and Barnabas went to preach in foreign lands, who did most of the talking? The spokesman was _____.

668. According to Paul's first letter to the Corinthians, "And now abideth faith, hope, charity, these three; but the greatest of these is _____."

669. John says Jesus carried his own cross, but Matthew, Mark, and Luke agree the cross was borne by _____ the Cyrenian.

670. Agrippa said to Paul: "Almost thou persuadest me to be a _____."

38. Analogies

The form here is A is to B as C is to _____. Your job is to figure the connection and determine D.

671. David : sling :: Samson : _____.

672. Shem : Noah ·· David : _____,

673. Manger : Jesus :: ark of bulrushes : _____.

674. Lazarus : Jesus :: Eutychus : _____.

675. Genesis : Malachi :: Matthew : _____.

39. Creation Days

On Day One, of course, God created light and darkness, Day and Night. On the seventh day, God rested. But what of the days in between? Can you match the days with what was created?

676. The sun, the moon, the stars   second day

677. Heaven   third day

678. Earth, seas, grass, herb yielding seed, tree yielding fruit   fourth day

679. Land animals and man   fifth day

680. Sea creatures and fowl   sixth day

40. More Complete the Quote

681. "And all the days of Methuselah were..."

682. "But his wife looked back from behind him, and she became...."

683. "I am Alpha and Omega...'

684. "Speak; for thy servant..."

685. "Peter saith unto him, Thou shalt never wash..."

686. "Greater love hath no man than this..."

687. "Eli, Eli..."

688. "Naked came I out of my mother's womb..."

689. "The Lord is my strength and..."

690. "By the rivers of Babylon, there we sat down; yea, we..."

691. "For whatsoever a man soweth..."

692. "Ye are the salt of the earth:..."

693. "Blessed are the poor in spirit:..."

694. "Who hath woe? who hath sorrow? who hath contentions? who hath babbling? who hath wounds without cause? who hath redness of eyes?..."

695. "The very hairs of your head..."

41. The Question Is, Why?

In this chapter you are told what happened; it's up to you to explain it.

696. Why did God drive Adam and Eve from the Garden of Eden?
    A. to punish them for eating the fruit
    B. to show them more of the world
    C. to keep them from eating of the tree of life and becoming immortal
    D. to separate them from the Cherubim

697. "And, behold, the vail of the temple was rent in twain, from the top to the bottom; and the earth did quake, and the rocks rent." Why?

698. Why did Joshua command the sun to stand still in the heavens?

699. Why, according to Jesus, was it all right for Mary of Bethany to anoint him with costly oil, rather than sell the oil for the benefit of the poor?

700. Why, in the parable of the ten virgins, were the five foolish virgins foolish?

701. Why, according to Elijah, would king Ahaziah, son of Ahab, not recover from his fall?

702. Why, after Ahaziah died, did his brother Jehoram rule Israel?

703. Why did David go to the camp, near where the Israelites were fighting the Philistines?

704. Why, according to Gamaliel, were the authorities better off allowing the apostles to preach about Jesus?

705. Why did Paul and Barnabas begin preaching to the Gentiles, when before they had preached only to the Jews?

706. Why did Paul travel to Macedonia?

707. Why did David arrange to have Uriah killed?
    A. because he wanted Uriah's armour
    B. because he wanted Uriah's wife
    C. because he wanted Uriah to be shown to be cowardly
    D. because Uriah had preached against the God of Israel

708. Why did Jesus say he had washed the disciples' feet?

709. Why were the other ten disciples upset with James and John?
    A. because they asked special favors
    B. because they were granted special favors
    C. because they had stopped observing the sabbath
    D. because they were talking of mutiny

710. Why did Haman want to kill the Jews?

711. Why did Paul live with Aquila and Priscilla in Corinth?

712. Why was Demetrius, the silversmith in Ephesus, worried about the preachings of Paul?

713. Why did Joseph take Mary and Jesus and flee to Egypt?

714. Why was Jesus disappointed when he returned to teach in the synagogue in his hometown?
    A. because he was not heeded
    B. because he was threatened with death
    C. because there were other powerful leaders
    D. because the synagogue was burned to the ground

715. Why did the Lord tell Ezekiel to prophesy against the shepherds of Israel?

716. Why did the apostle Thomas' actions give rise to the expression "Doubting Thomas"?

717. Why did the chief priests and Pharisees ask Pilate to guard the tomb of Jesus?

718. Why was the Ephraimites' speech problem fatal?

719. Why did Nebuchadnezzar fall upon his face and
worship Daniel?
   A. because he thought Daniel was God's son
   B. because Daniel told him of a dream he had
      forgotten, and interpreted it.
   C. because Daniel had defeated the lions
   D. because he was possessed by demons

720. "Jesus wept." (John 11:35) Why?

42. Hidden Words—Books of the Bible

721-755. See how many books of the Bible you can find named here. You should snare thirty-five, if you search diligently.

S	O	N	G	O	F	S	O	L	O	M	O	N	C	T	Y	E
N	R	C	A	M	O	S	S	E	L	C	I	N	O	R	H	C
A	U	O	L	C	J	E	N	A	N	D	Y	I	R	H	T	C
I	C	L	A	D	T	R	S	U	I	R	Y	N	I	E	O	L
N	S	O	T	A	E	S	T	H	E	R	U	C	N	I	M	E
O	M	S	I	N	V	D	I	S	T	B	E	T	T	T	I	S
L	L	S	A	I	E	R	U	O	O	N	F	O	H	Y	T	I
A	A	I	N	E	L	E	O	J	E	R	E	M	I	A	H	A
S	S	A	S	L	M	T	N	O	H	E	X	A	A	W	Y	S
S	P	N	C	O	B	E	U	N	A	S	O	R	N	K	O	T
E	N	S	L	U	I	P	A	A	C	C	D	K	S	H	R	E
H	A	B	A	K	K	U	K	H	I	H	U	B	A	A	O	S
T	S	W	E	R	B	E	H	N	M	E	S	A	H	R	M	J
E	T	S	N	A	I	S	E	H	P	E	L	C	E	R	Z	E
K	A	G	E	N	E	S	I	S	Y	L	E	I	K	E	Z	E
U	B	A	D	O	N	D	E	U	T	E	R	O	N	O	M	Y
L	E	U	M	A	S	N	O	I	T	A	T	N	E	M	A	L

43. Multiple Choice—New Testament

756. James, Joses, Simon, and Judas were, according to
     Matthew—
     A. secret disciples
     B. brethren of Jesus
     C. assistants to Paul
     D. wise men

757. At Jesus' first trial, which of the following did the elders
     do to him? (More than one.)
     A. convict him of blasphemy
     B. smite him with the palms of their hands
     C. tear his clothes
     D. spit on him

758. For the crucifixion, the soldiers removed the robe and
     dressed Jesus in—
     A. tattered rags
     B. his own clothes

C. the robe of Pilate

D. the skin of a lamb

759. Who witnessed Jesus' conversation with Elias and
Moses?
A. Peter and Bartholemew
B. Peter alone
C. Peter, James, and John
D. no one at all

760. Jesus felt favorably disposed toward anyone who gave
his disciples even—
A. a crust of bread
B. a cup of water
C. a single blessing
D. the time of day

761. When the rulers told Peter and John not to preach in
the name of Jesus, the two disciples—
A. said that God's orders were more powerful and
that they therefore would continue to preach in
his name
B. said they would obey, but then ignored their
pledge
C. said they would obey, but encouraged other
disciples to preach in his name
D. pretended to be deaf, so as to avoid confronta-
tion

762. What was Jesus doing when his disciples came to tell
him the stormy sea was threatening to drown them all?
A. preaching
B. praying
C. sleeping
D. talking with Simon Peter

763. When Herod heard of the fame of Jesus, he said his miracles must be the work of—
    A. the devil
    B. John the Baptist, risen from the dead
    C. only God himself
    D. the rumor mongers

764. When the Samaritans refused Jesus hospitality, what did the disciples James and John recommend?
    A. that they stone the Samaritans
    B. that they order fire to come down from heaven and consume them
    C. that Jesus ignore them and go elsewhere
    D. that Jesus ask God to persuade the Samaritans himself

765. After Jesus pointed to Judas Iscariot as the one who would betray him, Judas—
    A. fell on his knees and asked forgiveness
    B. threatened to have Jesus killed immediately
    C. asked for more lamb to eat
    D. left the room immediately

766. Which psalm did Paul cite to the Jews in the synagogue at Antioch?
    A. the first
    B. the twenty-third
    C. the fiftieth
    D. the second

767. In Jerusalem, Paul was seen with Trophimus, an Ephesian. The Jews thought that Paul had—
    A. taken him into the temple
    B. converted him
    C. paid him a sum of money
    D. brought him back from the dead

768. Which epistle was written to an "elect lady"?
    A. The First Epistle of John
    B. The Second Epistle of John
    C. The First Epistle of Peter
    D. The Second Epistle of Peter

769. What was Jesus doing while his parents searched for him in Jerusalem?
    A. discoursing with the doctors in the temple
    B. praying with the elders in the synagogue
    C. preaching on a street corner among the Gentiles
    D. sitting on a high hill alone

770. Referring to Jesus' disciples: "And the Pharisees said unto him, Behold, why do they on the sabbath day that which is not lawful?" Do what?
    A. fish
    B. pick corn
    C. commit adultery
    D. heal the sick

771. Who announced that John the Baptist, yet unborn, would "make ready a people prepared for the Lord"?
    A. Luke
    B. Elias
    C. Gabriel
    D. Zacharias

772. How did the shepherds react when they first saw the angel of the Lord, come to tell them of the birth of Jesus?
    A. uninterested
    B. drunk
    C. afraid
    D. overjoyed

115

773. John the Baptist compared himself to—
    A. a bridegroom
    B. a bridegroom's friend
    C. a judge
    D. a herald

774. When Jesus told the nobleman he would find his son healed at home, the nobleman—
    A. said, "I would that it were so, my Lord"
    B. said, "canst thou make such promises in the name of God?"
    C. asked Jesus to pray with him
    D. believed Jesus and went on his way

775. Jesus was on the cross—
    A. one hour
    B. two hours
    C. six hours
    D. twelve hours

44. The Last Letter

A quiz about characters whose names start with "Z."

776. Was Zacchaeus rich or poor?

777. Zebedee's relationship to the apostles James and John: _____.
    A. brother
    B. father
    C. teacher
    D. arch-enemy

778. Which king allowed the princes to put Jeremiah into a dungeon, where he sank in the mire?

779. Zilpah was a _____ to Leah.
    A. good friend
    B. sister
    C. handmaid
    D. mother-in-law

780. What did Zophar the Naamathite have in common with Eliphaz the Temanite and Bildad the Shuhite?

781. Either Zephaniah or Zechariah contains the prediction, "Behold, thy King cometh unto thee; he is just, and having salvation; lowly, and riding upon an ass, and upon a colt the foal of an ass." Which book?

782. Zechariah took two staves; one he named Beauty, the other _____.
    A. Beast
    B. Beautiful
    C. Haggai
    D. Bands

783. He became king by killing Elah, the king who reigned before him, but he himself reigned only seven days.

784. Zacharias and Elisabeth were the parents of _____.

785. These women, according to the Lord, "are haughty, and walk with stretched forth necks, and wanton eyes, walking and mincing as they go and making a tinkling with their feet." Who are they?

45. Final Potpourri

A miscellany of questions

786. What is the last line of the twenty-third Psalm?

787. What feature of their births did they have in common: Isaac and Samuel.

788. What did these two have in common: Peninnah and Hannah.

789. And what did Baalim and Ashtaroth have in common?

790. It was predicted: "For though thy people Israel be as the sand of the sea, yet a remnant of them shall return." By what prophet? Was it—
    A. Isaiah
    B. Elijah
    C. Jeremiah
    D. Deborah

791. It happened in the six-hundredth year of his life, in the second month, the seventeenth day of the month. Who was he and what happened?

792. What did Samson do that David also did, and Benaiah as well?
    A. each slew a lion
    B. each fasted seven days
    C. each was son of a king
    D. each was slain by a woman

793. "O praise the Lord, all ye nations: praise him, all ye people. For his merciful kindness is great toward us: and the truth of the Lord endureth for ever. Praise ye the Lord." What's distinctive about this quotation?

794. *Who* was directed by God to do *what* once a day for six days and seven times on the seventh day?

795. What famous line *follows* this line: "If ye then, being evil, know how to give good gifts unto your children, how much more shall your Father which is in heaven give good things to them that ask him?"

Answers

1. Titles

1. David. (1 Samuel 17)
2. Daniel. (Daniel 6)
3. Samson. (Judges 14-16)
4. Solomon. (1 Kings 3-11)
5. Job. (Job)

2. Complete the Quote

6. "... there was no room for them in the inn." (Luke 2:7)
7. "...TEKEL UPHARSIN." (Daniel 5:25)
8. "... for thou shalt find it after many days." (Ecclesiastes 11:1)
9. "... and he that believeth on me shall never thirst." (John 6:35)
10. "... save me, and I shall be saved." (Jeremiah 17:14)
11. "feed him"; "give him drink" (Romans 12:20)
12. "...O grave, where is thy victory?" (1 Corinthians 15:55)
13. "... there am I in the midst of them." (Matthew 18:20)
14. "... go, and sin no more." (John 8:11)
15. "... son is given...." (Isaiah 9:6)
16. "... a light unto my path." (Psalms 119:105)
17. "... who can be against us?" (Romans 8:31)
18. "... where thou lodgest, I will lodge: thy people shall be my people, and thy God my God: Where thou diest will I die, and there will I be buried...." (Ruth 1:16-17)
19. "... make you free." (John 8:32)
20. "... but few are chosen." (Matthew 22:14)

3. Multiple Choice—The Easy Test

21. A. (Matthew 27:28; Mark 15:17; John 19:2)
22. A. (Proverbs 1:7)
23. D. (Ecclesiastes 9:5)
24. B. (Matthew 26:48-49; Mark 14:44-46; Luke 22:47-48)
25. B. (Isaiah 57:21)
26. C. (Daniel 5:1-5)
27. B. (Jonah 1:15)
28. B. (Ezekiel 37:8-10)
29. B. (1 Samuel 17:50-51)
30. B. (Exodus 17:6)
31. A. (Genesis 19:30)
32. B. (Genesis 25:25)
33. C. (Genesis 32:28)
34. D. (Genesis 6:14)
35. A. (John 11:14-17)
36. A. (Genesis 22:10)
37. D. (Genesis 2:17)
38. D. (Genesis 8:20)
39. C.
40. C. (Colossians 4:14)

4. True or False?

41. False—"she called for a man, and she caused him to shave off the seven locks of his head...." (Judges 16:19)
42. False. (Jonah 1:12-15)
43. False—he made a strong east wind divide the waters. (Exodus 14:21)
44. True. (Joshua 3:15-17)
45. False—it was the people's great shout. (Joshua 6:20)
46. False—for about one day. (Joshua 10:13)
47. False. (Deuteronomy 32:48-52)
48. True. (2 Samuel 13:18)

49. False—it measured smaller. (Genesis 6:15; 2 Chronicles 3:3)
50. False—a whirlwind took him, in a flaming chariot drawn by flaming horses. (2 Kings 2:11)
51. False—he lived another 140 years. (Job 42:16)
52. False—Darius in fact sympathized with Daniel, but he had to abide by a law he had signed prohibiting petition to anyone but the king for thirty days. (Daniel 6:12-16)
53. True. (Deuteronomy 23:24-25)
54. True. (Daniel 3:14-30)
55. True. (Proverbs 1:7)

5. Dreams

56. Jacob. (Genesis 28:10-12)
57. Pharoah. (Genesis 41:17-20)
58. Nebuchadnezzar. (Daniel 2:28-32)
59. Joseph. (Genesis 37:5-9)
60. Abimelech. (Genesis 20:2-3)

6. Moses

61. False—his mother kept him for three months, *then* hid him by the river. (Exodus 2:2-3)
62. His own mother. (Exodus 2:8-9)
63. B. (Exodus 12:37)
64. C. (Exodus 19:16)
65. True. (Exodus 34:1)
66. "Flee before thee." (Numbers 10:35)
67. D. (Numbers 20:10-12)
68. A. (Deuteronomy 26:1-2)
69. "Ye shall hearken." (Deuteronomy 18:15)
70. "In a valley in the land of Moab." (Deuteronomy 34:5-6)

7. What Book Does It Come From?

71. B. (Exodus 3:2-4)
72. B. (Matthew 5:5)
73. A. (1 John 4:8)
74. A. (Mark 16:19)
75. C. (Genesis 3:19)
76. D. (Philippians 2:10)
77. A. (John 3:16)
78. D. (John 6:51)
79. D. (Exodus 20:2-17)
80. C. (Leviticus 11)
81. B. (Deuteronomy 27:18)
82. C. (Judges 9:8-15)
83. D. (Ecclesiastes 1:9)
84. B. (Proverbs 31:10-31)
85. C. (John 18:5, 8)
86. B. (1 Samuel 5:1-4)
87. C. (1 Chronicles 22:6-7; 28:10-20)
88. A. (Isaiah 7:14)
89. A. (Ezekiel 18:20)
90. C. (Nahum 1:2)
91. B. (Isaiah 11:6)
92. D. (Jeremiah 13:23)
93. A. (Galatians 5:19-23)
94. C. (Romans 12:18)
95. A. (Ephesians 6:1)

8. Places

96. Sinai. (Exodus 24:12-16)
97. Nebo. (Deuteronomy 34:1)
98. Hor. (Numbers 20:27-28)
99. Moriah. (Genesis 22:2)
100. Ararat. (Genesis 8:4)
101. Tarsus. (Acts 9:11)

102. It was the site of the tower of Babel. (Genesis 11:2-9)
103. Gilgal. (Joshua 5:10)
104. Hebron. (Joshua 14:13)
105. In Sychar, a city of Samaria. (John 4:5-7)
106. A. (Esther 1:2)
107. Patmos. (Revelation 1:9)
108. Bethany. (John 11:14-18; 43-44)
109. Uz. (Job 1:1)
110. D. (Jonah 1:1-2; 3:2-3)
111. B. (Joshua 24:32)
112. Melita. (Acts 27:41-44; 28:1)
113. Potter's field. (Matthew 27:3,7)
114. Calvary. (Matthew 27:33; Mark 15:22; Luke 23:33; John 19:17)
115. B. (Acts 8:5)
116. On the road to Damascus. (Acts 9:1-18)
117. On the roof. (Acts 10:9-17)
118. Antioch. (Acts 11:26)
119. In the river Jordan. (Matthew 3:1,6; Mark 1:4-5)
120. Under the fig tree. (John 1:48)
121. Bethesda. (John 5:2-9)
122. Thy closet. (Matthew 6:6)
123. He sat in a ship in the sea; the crowd stood on shore. (Matthew 13:2; Mark 4:1)
124. Gethsemane. (Matthew 26:36, 50; Mark 14:32, 46)
125. In the valley of Elah. (1 Samuel 17:2-4, 50)
126. Damascus. (Isaiah 17:1)
127. Babylon. (Jeremiah 25:9-12)
128. Chebar. (Ezekiel 1:1)
129. A. (Daniel 3:1, 14, 19-21)
130. The land of Nod. (Genesis 4:16)

9. All in the Family

131. David; Bathsheba. (2 Samuel 12:24)
132. Haman. (Esther 3:1)
133. Father of king David. (1 Samuel 16:11-13)
134. Great-grandson (son of Enoch, who was son of Cain). (Genesis 4:18)
135. Noah. (Genesis 5:25-29)
136. Nephew. (Genesis 12:5)
137. A. (Genesis 22:21)
138. Nephew (Genesis 28:1-2) and son-in-law (Genesis 29:16-28)
139. Cousins. (Esther 2:5-7)
140. Elimelech, her husband. (Ruth 2:1)
141. His mother and his great-aunt. (Exodus 6:20)
142. His sisters, Mary and Martha. (John 11:1-3)
143. Greek. (Acts 16:1)
144. Uriah. (2 Samuel 11:1-17)
145. "Whosoever shall do the will of God." (Mark 3:35)
146. Rachel. (Genesis 29:5-6)
147. Saul. (1 Samuel 18:26-27)
148. Amittai. (Jonah 1:1)
149. Joash. (Judges 6:11)
150. Enoch. (Genesis 4:17)

151. ABIGAIL
152. AHOLAH
153. AHOLIBAH
154. ANNA
155. BASHEMATH
156. DEBORAH
157. ESTHER
158. EVE
159. GOMER
160. HAGAR
161. HANNAH
162. HERODIAS
163. JAEL
164. JEZEBEL
165. JOCHEBED
166. JUDITH
167. KETURAH
168. LEAH
169. MARTHA
170. MARY
171. MERAB
172. MICHAL
173. MIRIAM
174. NAOMI
175. ORPAH
176. PENINNAH
177. RACHEL
178. REBEKA
179. RUTH
180. SARAH
181. SHUAH
182. TABITHA
183. TAMAR
184. VASHTI
185. ZILPAH

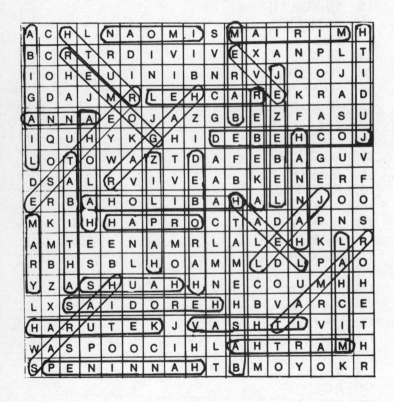

186. Paul. (Romans 6:23)
187. Jesus. (Luke 4:24)
188. Jesus. (Matthew 7:20)
189. Balaam. (Numbers 23:16;23)
190. Solomon. (1 Kings 3:25)
191. Samuel. (1 Samuel 12:2)
192. Hannah. (1 Samuel 2:2)
193. John the Baptist. (Matthew 3:1-2)
194. Paul. (2 Timothy 4:6-7)
195. Job. (Job 1:21)
196. Paul. (1 Thessalonians 4:16-17)
197. The shepherds. (Luke 2:15)
198. Paul. (1 Corinthians 13:11)
199. Jesus. (Mark 4:37-39)
200. Jesus. (Mark 9:31)
201. Pharaoh. (Exodus 1:22)
202. Moses. (Exodus 4:10)
203. Moses. (Exodus 32:26)
204. Nathaniel. (John 1:49)
205. Jeremiah. (Lamentations 1:1)
206. To Hannah, who had asked the Lord for a child. (1 Samuel 1:15-17)
207. To the lame beggar outside the temple. (Acts 3:1-6)
208. To Jesus. (John 3:3-4)
209. To his ass. (Numbers 22:29)
210. To Joshua. (Joshua 5:15)
211. Cain to God. (Genesis 4:9)
212. Judas Iscariot to the chief priests. (Matthew 26:14-15)
213. Jephthah to the elders of Gilead. (Judges 11:9)
214. God to Moses and Aaron. (Leviticus 11:1-7)
215. The angel Gabriel to Mary. (Luke 1:26-28)
216. About Jesus. (Mark 3:7, 22)
217. About Absalom, his son. (2 Samuel 18:33)

218. About an earlier son, who was taken from him by the Lord as punishment for sin. (2 Samuel 12:18-23)
219. About Saul and his son, Jonathan. (2 Samuel 1:17, 19, 25, 27)
220. About Job. (Job 1:8)

12. Who's Who

221. Job. (Job 1:14-19)
222. John the Baptist. (John 1:26-27)
223. David. (1 Samuel 16:23)
224. Solomon. (1 Kings 4:30-31)
225. Aaron. (Exodus 32:3-6)
226. Moses. (Deuteronomy 34:10)
227. Absalom. (2 Samuel 15:1-13)
228. Caesar Augustus. (Luke 2:1-5)
229. Peter. (Matthew 14:29-31)
230. Ezekiel. (Ezekiel 1:3-6)
231. Seth. (Genesis 4:25)
232. Gideon. (Judges 7:15-16)
233. Peter. (Matthew 26:33-34; Mark 14:29-30; Luke 22:34; John 13:37-38)
234. Jacob. (Genesis 32:24)
235. Pilate. (Matthew 27:24)
236. Barnabas and Saul. (Acts 13:1-5)
237. Paul. (Acts 21:10-11)
238. Joshua. (Joshua 1:1-9)
239. Daniel. (Daniel 5:17, 25-28)
240. Isaiah. (Isaiah 20:3)

13. It Didn't Happen

241. D. (Matthew 27:51-53)
242. A. (Acts 2:1-4)
243. D. (Matthew 16:13-14; Mark 8:27-28; Luke 9:18-19)
244. D. (Ecclesiastes 3:1-8)
245. C. (Luke 7:37-38)

14. Husbands and Wives

246. Sarah. (Genesis 17:15)
247. Milcah. (Genesis 11:29)
248. Rachel. (Genesis 29:28)
249. Jael. (Judges 4:17)
250. Ruth. (Ruth 4:13)

15. Animals

251. B. (Judges 14:5-6)
252. Asses. (1 Samuel 9:3)
253. Jacob, to Esau. (Genesis 32:13-15)
254. It talked with its master. (Numbers 22:28)
255. A lion and a bear. (1 Samuel 17:34-36)
256. The lamb.
257. The kid.
258. The young lion. } (Isaiah 11:6-7)
259. The bear.
260. The ox.
261. A mule. (2 Samuel 18:9)
262. A dead lion. (Ecclesiastes 9:4)
263. C. (Mark 5:13)
264. Sheep. (Matthew 12:11)
265. Those who had accused Daniel and their wives and children. (Daniel 6:24)
266. A. (Jeremiah 17:11)
267. Raven. (Genesis 8:6-7)
268. An ass. (Matthew 21:1-10)
269. Camel. (Matthew 19:24; Mark 10:25)
270. B. (Genesis 2:19-20)

271. HE PLAYS BANJO BADLY, BUT SINGS WELL.
272. TIPS, ALMS, INHERITANCES: ALL ARE TAXABLE.
273. MAN NAMED EUGENE, SISTER NAMED JUDITH. NO FURTHER INFO.
274. I'M AT THE WINDOW LOOKING OUT ONTO THE LAWN.
275. I AM A FRANCOPHILE, MONSIEUR. ET VOUS?
276. NUR EINMAL? ACH! ICH BIN ENTTÄUSCHT!
277. HE NEVER WENT OUT WITHOUT TAKING A WALKING STICK.
278. AFTER VISITING JORDAN, I ELECTED TO GO HOME.
279. YES, A MOST INTERESTING BOOK, I THOUGHT.
280. WEATHER FORECAST: STORM. ARK NEEDS REPAIRS. PLEASE ADVISE.
281. ISN'T IT USELESS TO PROTEST TO THEM?
282. THE OLDEST HERITAGE ISN'T NECESSARILY THE BEST.
283. A BUSHEL OF APPLES, ALL RIPE: TERRIFIC!
284. IS JAM ESSENTIAL TO A PEANUT BUTTER SANDWICH?
285. THOSE AREN'T THE ONES I ASKED FOR.
286. A COMIC, A HOLLYWOOD AGENT, AND A PRODUCER HAD LUNCH.
287. ANNA, HUMBLE ANNA, DEAR SWEET ANNA!
288. "THIS TIME THE BREW SHOULD HAVE ITS EFFECT," SAID THE WITCH.
289. HE ALMOST LOST HIS FEZ, RACING UP THE STEPS.
290. THAT'S THE "MONA LISA," I—AH—THINK. OR IS IT "GUERNICA"?

17. Which Comes First?

291. Eve's. (Genesis 3:6)
292. Cain. (Genesis 4:1-2)
293. The Flood. (Genesis 6-9, 11)
294. Esau. (Genesis 25:25-26)
295. Frogs. (Exodus 8:1-18)
296. Locusts. (Exodus 10:4-23)
297. "Thou shalt not kill." (Exodus 20:13, 15)
298. "Thou shalt not commit adultery." (Exodus 20:14, 16)
299. Omri. (1 Kings 16:16, 29)
300. Amaziah (2 Chronicles 26:1; 2 Kings 15:1)
301. Daniel in the lions' den. (Daniel 6, Jonah 1-2)
302. The commandment to love God. (Matthew 22:37-39; Mark 12:29-31)
303. Exodus.
304. Psalms.
305. Colossians.

18. Which King...?

306. Herod. (Matthew 2:16)
307. The king of Nineveh. (Jonah 3:6)
308. Saul. (1 Samuel 28:7-11)
309. Nebuchadnezzar. (Daniel 4:33)
310. Achish the king of Gath. (1 Samuel 21:12-15)
311. Og king of Bashan. (Deuteronomy 3:11)
312. Jehoiakim. (Jeremiah 36:29-31)
313. Solomon. (1 Kings 11:4-9)
314. Ahab. (1 Kings 16:33)
315. Ahasuerus. (Esther 6:1)
316. Rehoboam. (1 Kings 11:43)
317. Herod. (Luke 13:31-32)
318. David. (Acts 13:22)
319. Ahasuerus. (Esther 2:16-17)
320. Ahab. (1 Kings 22:20, 30)

19. Words of God

321. "Reason together." (Isaiah 1:18)
322. "Son of man, can these bones live?" (Ezekiel 37:3)
323. Zechariah (Zechariah 8:4-5)
324. "See visions." (Joel 2:28)
325. Yes—"This is my beloved Son, in whom I am well pleased" (Matthew 3:17) and "This is my beloved Son; hear him" (Mark 9:7; Luke 9:35)
326. A. (Genesis 12:1)
327. C. (Exodus 3:14)
328. A. (Joshua 1:6, 9, 18)
329. D. (Job 40:9)
330. B. (Genesis 3:14)

20. Hidden Words—Places

331. ASSOS
332. BEREA
333. BETHEL
334. BETHLEHEM
335. CALVARY
336. CANAAN
337. CAPERNAUM
338. CARMEL
339. CYPRUS
340. DAMASCUS
341. EBAL
342. EGYPT
343. GALATIA
344. GALILEE

345. GAZA
346. GETHSEMANE
347. GILGAL
348. HEBRON
349. JERICHO
350. JERUSALEM
351. JOPPA
352. JORDAN
353. KIRJATHJEARIM
354. MACEDONIA
355. MORIAH
356. NAIN
357. NAZARETH
358. NEBO
359. NOB
360. PHRYGIA
361. SALAMIS
362. UR
363. ZIN
364. ZION
365. ZIPHRON

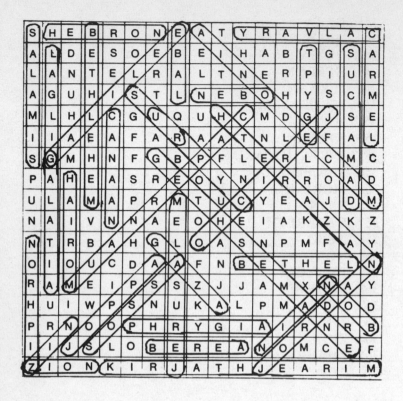

21. One-Word Answers—Old Testament

366. Skins. (Genesis 3:21)
367. East. (Genesis 3:24)
368. Right. (Exodus 15:6)
369. Water. (Exodus 17)
370. Blue. (Numbers 15:38-39)
371. Tenth. (Deuteronomy 23:2)
372. Saul. (1 Samuel 9:1-2)
373. Brass. (1 Samuel 17:4-5, 38)

374. Tamar. (2 Samuel 13:10-32)
375. Judge. (1 Kings 3:9-15)
376. Young. (1 Kings 12:1-14)
377. Dogs. (1 Kings 21:17-19; 22:37-38)
378. Bald. (2 Kings 2:22-23)
379. Bears. (2 Kings 2:24)
380. Rich. (Job 1:1-3)
381. Preacher. (Ecclesiastes)
382. Left; right. (Song of Solomon 2:6)
383. Rechabites. (Jeremiah 35:1-2, 5-10)
384. Israel. (Amos 4:12)
385. Humbly. (Micah 6:8)

22. Occupations

386. Carpenter. (Matthew 13:55)
387. Fisherman. (Matthew 4:18; Mark 1:16; Luke 5:1-3)
388. Tiller of the ground. (Genesis 4:2)
389. Shepherd. (1 Samuel 16:11-13)
390. Hunter. (Genesis 25:27)
391. Tentmaker. (Acts 18:1-3)
392. Keeper of sheep. (Genesis 4:2)
393. Herdman. (Amos 7:14)
394. Cupbearer to the king. (Nehemiah 1:11)
395. Beggar. (Luke 16:20)
396. Harlot. (Joshua 2:1)
397. Scribe. (2 Kings 18:18)
398. Servant. (2 Kings 4:12)
399. Handmaid to Sarai. (Genesis 16:1)
400. Midwife. (Exodus 1:15)

23. How Did They Die?

401. Haman. (Esther 7:10)
402. The man who gathered sticks on the sabbath. (Numbers 15:32-36)
403. Jezebel. (2 Kings 9:30-33)
404. Judas Iscariot. (Matthew 27:3, 5)
405. Ananias. (Acts 5:1-6)
406. Stephen. (Acts 7:55-60; 8:1-2)
407. Herod. (Acts 12:21-23)
408. Eli. (1 Samuel 4:16-18)
409. Saul. (1 Samuel 31:1-5)
410. Samson. (Judges 16:29-30)
411. The Pharaoh's chief baker. (Genesis 40:18-22)
412. The ten members of the search party. (Numbers 14:36- 37)
413. Balaam. (Numbers 31:8)
414. Eglon king of Moab. (Judges 3:14-25)
415. Sisera, the Canaanite captain. (Judges 4:18-21)
416. Eutychus. (Acts 20:9)
417. Agag the king of the Amalekites. (1 Samuel 15:32-33)
418. Uzzah, the man who touched the ark. (2 Samuel 6:6-7)
419. Absalom. (2 Samuel 18:9-15)
420. Nadab and Abihu, the bad sons of Aaron. (Leviticus 10:1-2)

24. Opening Words

421. Deuteronomy
422. Exodus
423. Genesis
424. Numbers
425. Leviticus
426. Ruth
427. Esther
428. I Kings
429. Psalms

430. 1 Chronicles.
431. John.
432. Mark.
433. Acts.
434. Matthew.
435. Luke.

25. Last Words

436. Genesis.
437. John.
438. Ecclesiastes.
439. Psalms.
440. Song of Solomon.

26. Food and Drink

441. Milk and honey. (Numbers 13:27)
442. A., B., and C. (Numbers 13:23)
443. "For thy stomach's sake and thine often infirmities." (1 Timothy 5:23)
444. C. (Genesis 18:6-8)
445. Venison. (Genesis 25:28)
446. A. (Genesis 25:34)
447. Bread. (Genesis 37:25)
448. Bitter herbs. (Exodus 12:3-8)
449. Manna. (Exodus 16:14-15)
450. Quail. (Numbers 11:31-33)
451. The ravens; bread and flesh, twice a day. (1 Kings 17:1, 6)
452. Butter and honey. (Isaiah 7:14-15)
453. C. (Ezekiel 2:9-10; 3:1-2)
454. A diet of water and pulse was superior to eating the king's meat and drinking his wine. (Daniel 1:11-16)

455. C. (Matthew 3:1-4; Mark 1:6)
456. Broiled fish; honeycomb. (Luke 24:41-43)
457. Apples. (Numbers 11:5)
458. Wine. (Proverbs 23:31-32)
459. Fine flour; meal. (1 Kings 4:22)
460. B. (Leviticus 2:13)
461. B. (Judges 4:19)
462. A. (Nahum 3:12)
463. D. (Numbers 17:8)
464. Dry and moldy. (Joshua 9:5, 12)
465. D. (Colossians 4:6)

27. More Who's Who

466. Jeremiah. (Jeremiah 20:1-2)
467. Azariah (also called Uzziah). (2 Kings 15:1-2; 2 Chronicles 26:1-3)
468. Jotham, the youngest. (Judges 9:4-5)
469. Jonathan, Saul's son. (1 Samuel 19:1-6)
470. Elijah. (1 Kings 17:17-22)
471. Elisha. (2 Kings 2:19-22)
472. Simeon. (Luke 2:25-30)
473. The son of man, Jesus. (Luke 9:58)
474. Zacchaeus. (Luke 19:2-4)
475. Malchus. (John 18:10)
476. Joseph of Arimathaea. (Matthew 27:57-58; Mark 15:43-46; Luke 23:50-53; John 19:38-42)
477. John Mark. (Acts 15:37-39)
478. Caleb the son of Jephunneh and Joshua the son of Nun. (Numbers 14:6-9)
479. Eleazar. (Numbers 20:25-28)
480. Achan. (Joshua 7:1-11)
481. Ehud. (Judges 3:15-16)
482. Reuben. (Genesis 37:21-22)
483. Enoch. (Genesis 5:22)
484. Potiphar. (Genesis 37:36)
485. Jesus. (1 Peter 2:21-23)

28. Numbers

486. Nine hundred sixty-nine. (Genesis 5:27)
487. Three hundred. (Genesis 6:15)
488. Ten thousands. (1 Samuel 18:7-8)
489. Fifty. (2 Kings 2: 11. 17)
490. A. (Deuteronomy 34:7)
491. Three; three. (Jonah 1:17)
492. Three. (Acts 9:8-9)
493. Four hundred ninety (seventy times seven). (Matthew 18:21-22)
494. Seventy. (Luke 10:1)
495. Five of each. (Matthew 25:1-2)
496. Three. (Matthew 26:60-61; Mark 14:57-58)
497. Thirty. (2 Samuel 5:4)
498. C. (1 Kings 18:22)
499. Seven. (2 Kings 4:35)
500. The Jews who returned to Jerusalem to build a temple during the reign of Cyrus the king of Persia. (Ezra 1:2-3; 2:1. 64-67)
501. A. (Joshua 24:32)
502. Six. (John 2:6)
503. One tenth of all that God gave him. (Genesis 28:22)
504. Twelve; threescore and ten. (Exodus 15:27)
505. Seventy. (Numbers 11:16-17)
506. Three. (1 Samuel 3:4-8)
507. C. (Numbers 35:6-7)
508. Fifty thousand seventy. (1 Samuel 6:19)
509. Seventeen. (Genesis 37:2-3)
510. Seven. (Genesis 7:2)
511. Twice seven, or fourteen. (Genesis 29:18-28)
512. D. (Genesis 7:24)
513. Three. (Genesis 8:8-12)
514. Ten. (Genesis 18:32)

515. One hundred fifty. (Psalms)
516. Threescore years and ten. (Psalms 90:10)
517. Eighteen thousand. (Ezekiel 48:31-35)
518. A. (Luke 1:56-57)
519. Three days. (Luke 2:43-46)
520. Ten; all ten; one. (Luke 17:11-18)

29. The Number Forty

521. Forty; forty. (Genesis 7:12)
522. Forty. (Exodus 16:35)
523. Forty. (Acts 7:29-30)
524. Forty; forty. (Exodus 34:27-28)
525. Forty. (Numbers 13:25)
526. Forty. (Matthew 4:1-2; Mark 1:9, 13; Luke 4:1-2)
527. Forty; forty. (1 Kings 19:8-9)
528. Forty. (Jonah 3:4)
529. Thirty. (Matthew 26: 14-15)
530. Forty. (Acts 7:22-24)
531. Forty. (2 Samuel 5:4)
532. Forty. (1 Kings 11:42)
533. Forty. (Acts 1:3, 9)
534. Seven. (2 Kings 11:21)
535. Forty. (Acts 23:12-13)

30. The Miracles of Jesus

536. Changing water into wine at a marriage ceremony in Cana. (John 2:3-11)
537. From a lad. (John 6:9)
538. C. (Matthew 9:27-30)
539. The daughter. (Mark 5:22-23. 35-43)
540. The son of a widow; in Nain. (Luke 7:11-14)
541. The servant of the centurion. (Luke 7:2-10)
542. First the net broke; then Simon and his partners managed to get the fish aboard two ships and the two began to sink. (Luke 5:4-7)
543. A. (John 4:52-53)
544. B. (Mark 1:30-31)
545. It was done on the sabbath. (John 5:2-16)

31. The Words of Jesus

546. "... in the name of the Father. and of the Son. and of the Holy Ghost." (Matthew 28:19)
547. Den; thieves. (Matthew 21:13; Mark 11:17; Luke 19:46)
548. "... that ye be not judged." (Matthew 7:1)
549. "... neither cast ye your pearls before swine. lest they trample them under their feet. and turn again and rend you." (Matthew 7:6)
550. "... seek. and ye shall find; knock. and it shall be opened unto you." (Matthew 7:7)
551. "... for they shall see God." (Matthew 5:8)
552. "... pluck it out. and cast it from thee." (Matthew 5:29)
553. David. (Revelation 22:16)
554. "... John the Baptist." (Luke 7:28)
555. "... weep not for me. but weep for yourselves, and for your children." (Luke 23:28)
556. Saul. (Acts 9:4-5)
557. Peter. (Matthew 16:23; Mark 8:33)
558. The twelve disciples. (Luke 6:20)

559. The tempter (Satan), in answer to a suggestion that he change stones into bread. (Matthew 4:3-4; Luke 4:3-4)
560. Peter. (Matthew 14:29-31)
561. Nicodemus. (John 3:9-10, 16)
562. One of the Pharisees. (Matthew 22:34-37)
563. The twelve disciples. (Luke 9:3)
564. A messenger from Jairus, a ruler of the synagogue, whose only daughter had died. (Luke 8:41, 49-50)
565. Peter and Andrew. (Matthew 4:18-19)
566. On sand. (Matthew 7:24-27)
567. That if Satan be divided against himself he cannot stand. (Matthew 12:25-26; Mark 3:24-26; Luke 11:17-18)
568. B. (John 8:57-58)
569. At the end of the world, they will be cast "into a furnace of fire: there shall be wailing and gnashing of teeth." (Matthew 13:40-42)
570. "A certain woman, which had an issue of blood twelve years"; she was healed. (Mark 5:25-34)
571. His disciples were frightened to see him walk on water and he was trying to calm them. (Matthew 14:26-27)
572. "Both shall fall into the ditch." (Matthew 15:14)
573. "... fulfilled in your ears." (Luke 4:14-21)
574. C. (Matthew 9:9; Luke 5:27)
575. C. (Matthew 6:1-4)
576. The devil. (John 8:44)
577. True. (Matthew 6:14)
578. "The good shepherd giveth his life for the sheep." (John 10:11)
579. Shall be exalted. (Luke 18:14)
580. The adultress. (John 8:4-7)
581. Paul. (Acts 20:35-37)
582. The parable of the servant who owed ten thousand talents to his master. (Matthew 18:23-25)
583. False. (Matthew 6:8)
584. A. (Luke 10:30-35)
585. After. (Luke 23:33-34)

32. Multiple Choice—Old Testament

586. D. (Daniel 3:28-29)
587. C. (Ezekiel 14:12-20)
588. A. (Genesis 41:42)
589. A. (Ecclesiastes 10:8)
590. C. (Isaiah 53:7)
591. D. (1 Kings 18:27)
592. D. (2 Kings 9:20)
593. B. (2 Kings 18-19)
594. B. (1 Samuel 8:1-5)
595. C. (1 Kings 6:7)
596. D. (Joshua 2:12-13)
597. A. (Judges 6:11-16)
598. C. (Numbers 26:65)
599. B. (Genesis 45:3)
600. C. (Exodus 7:17)
601. C. (Genesis 16:1-3)
602. B. (Genesis 5:32; 6:10)
603. C. (1 Samuel 21:12-15)
604. B. (Job 38:1)
605. B. (Lamentations)

33. Women in the Bible

606. D. (Numbers 12:1)
607. Jezebel. (1 Kings 16:30-31; 21:23)
608. B. (Numbers 12:10)
609. Rachel, wife of Jacob. (Genesis 35:18-19)
610. The wife of Potiphar, Joseph's master in Egypt. (Genesis 39:1-20)
611. Rahab. (Joshua 2:1-6)
612. A. (Judges 11:30-40)
613. That he should have nothing to do with it, because she had received warnings in her dreams. (Matthew 27:17, 19)
614. Sweet spices, for anointing his body. (Mark 16:1; Luke 23:55-56, 24:1)

615. The mother of Samson. (Judges 13:3-5, 24)
616. C. (Ruth 1:2-4)
617. Mary. (Luke 1:46-48)
618. Drunk. (1 Samuel 1:13)
619. She laid a dummy of David in the bed and told them that her husband was sick, gving him time to flee. (1 Samuel 19:12-18)
620. B. (1 Kings 10:1-10)
621. Anna. (Luke 2:22-24, 36)
622. The daughter of Herodias. (Matthew 14:6-11)
623. His queen, Vashti. (Esther 1:17)
624. A. (Proverbs 31:1, 4)
625. Aholah and Aholibah; sisters. (Ezekiel 23:1-4)

34. Other Names

626. A. (Genesis 17:5)
627. C. (Genesis 17:15)
628. C. (Acts 13:9)
629. D. (Esther 2:7)
630. A. (Daniel 1:7)

35. Biblical Brothers

631. Andrew. (Matthew 4:18; Mark 1:16; John 6:8)
632. John. (Matthew 4:21; Mark 1:19; Luke 5:10)
633. Abihu. (Leviticus 10:1)
634. Benjamin. (Genesis 42:4)
635. Seth. (Genesis 4:1, 25)

36. Yes or No?

636. Yes. (Mark 16:9; John 20:1, 11-18)
637. Yes. (John 2:1-11)
638. No—it was Paul. (Acts 28:3-5)
639. Yes. (Matthew 6:13)
640. Yes. (Luke 1:13, 59-60)
641. No—the number is unstated. (Matthew 2:1-12)
642. Yes. (Matthew 5:28)
643. No. (Matthew 7:18)
644. No—he told him, "Go home to thy friends, and tell them how great things the Lord hath done for thee, and hath had compassion on thee." (Mark 5:19)
645. Yes. (Matthew 6:9-13; Luke 11:2-4)
646. No—he said to love God is the greatest. (Matthew 22:36-39; Mark 12:28-31)
647. No—he gave back the silver. (Matthew 27:3)
648. Yes—blood and water. (John 19:34)
649. Yes. (Acts 16:27-33)
650. No—they went into the synagogues. (Acts 13:2, 5)

37. One-Word Answers—New Testament

651. Truth. (John 1:17)
652. Dove. (Matthew 3:16; Mark 1:10; Luke 3:22; John 1:32)
653. Soul. (Matthew 16:26)
654. Spittle. (John 9:6-7)
655. Sabbath. (John 9:14)
656. Think. (Luke 12:40)
657. Blindness. (Mark 10:46-52)
658. Fig. (Matthew 21:19-22)
659. Son. (Matthew 22:1-3)
660. Penny. (Mark 12:14-15; Luke 20:22-24)
661. Sleeping. (Matthew 26:40-41)

662. Ear. (John 18:10)
663. Robber. (Mark 15:7; Luke 23:18-19; John 18:40)
664. Two. (Matthew 27:38; Mark 15:27; Luke 23:32; John 19:18)
665. Gardener. (John 20:1, 14-15)
666. Land. (Acts 5:1-3)
667. Paul. (Acts 14:12)
668. Charity. (1 Corinthians 13:13)
669. Simon. (Matthew 27:32; Mark 15:21; Luke 23:26; John 19:16-17)
670. Christian. (Acts 26:28)

38. Analogies

671. Jawbone of an ass. (weapon) (1 Samuel 17:40, 49; Judges 15:15-16)
672. Jesse. (son and father) (Genesis 5:32; 1 Samuel 16:11-13)
673. Moses. (sleeping place as ihfant) (Luke 2:7; Exodus 2:3)
674. Paul. (raised the dead) (John 11:43-44; Acts 20:9-12)
675. Revelation. (first and last books)

39. Creation Days

676. Fourth day.
677. Second day.
678. Third day. } (Genesis 1)
679. Sixth day.
680. Fifth day.

40. More Complete the Quote

681. "... nine hundred sixty and nine years: and he died."
    (Genesis 5:27)
682. "... a pillar of salt." (Genesis 19:26)
683. "... the beginning and the ending." (Revelation 1:8)
684. "... heareth." (1 Samuel 3:10)
685. "... my feet." (John 13:8)
686. "... that a man lay down his life for his friends." (John 15:13)
687. "... lama, sabachthani?" (Matthew 27:46)
688. "... and naked shall I return thither." (Job 1:21)
689. "... my shield." (Psalms 28:7)
690. "... wept, when we remembered Zion." (Psalms 137:1)
691. "... that shall he also reap." (Galatians 6:7)
692. "... but if the salt have lost his savour, wherewith shall it be salted?" (Matthew 5:13)
693. "... for theirs is the kingdom of heaven." (Matthew 5:3)
694. "... They that tarry long at the wine; they that go to seek mixed wine." (Proverbs 23:29-30)
695. "... are all numbered." (Matthew 10:30; Luke 12:7)

41. The Question Is, Why?

696. C. (Genesis 3:22-23)
697. Because Jesus died on the cross. (Matthew 27:50-51)
698. Because darkness would have let the Jews' enemies escape during a big battle. Extra light hours let Joshua win a big victory. (Joshua 6-8)
699. Because Jesus was on earth for but a short time, while the poor are here for always. (Matthew 26:6-11; Mark 14:3-7; John 12:1-8)
700. Because they brought with them lamps but no oil. (Matthew 25:1-3)
701. Because he appealed not to the God of Israel but to Baalzebub the god of Ekron. (2 Kings 1:15-16)

702. Because Ahaziah had no son. (2 Kings 1:17)
703. To bring food to his three brothers, who were soldiers, and to see how they were doing. (1 Samuel 17:17-20)
704. Because if their teaching was the work of men it would amount to nothing, and if it was the work of God it could not be overthrown. (Acts 5:34, 38-39)
705. Because the Jews didn't believe them. (Acts 13:46)
706. Because he had a vision in the night of a Macedonian asking him to come and help. (Acts 16:9-10)
707. B. (2 Samuel 11:2-17)
708. "For I have given you an example, that ye should do as I have done to you." (John 13:14-15)
709. A. (Matthew 20:21, 24; Mark 10:35, 41)
710. Because a Jew (Mordecai) refused to bow to him. (Esther 3:2, 5-6)
711. Because they were tentmakers, a trade he shared with them. (Acts 18:1-3)
712. Because the silversmiths' livelihood depended on orders to create silver shrines for the worship of Diana. (Acts 19:24-27)
713. Because the angel of the Lord appeared to him in a dream and warned that king Herod wanted to destroy the child. (Matthew 2:13)
714. A. (Mark 6:1-6)
715. Because they were feeding and caring for themselves and not their flocks. (Ezekiel 34:1-5)
716. Because he said he wouldn't believe Jesus had risen until he touched him and verified it himself. (John 20:24-25)
717. Because they feared his disciples might steal the body at night and tell people he had risen from the dead. (Matthew 27:62-64)
718. Because their inability to pronounce the "sh" sound gave away their identities and they were slain. (Judges 12:6)
719. B. (Daniel 2:31-46)
720. Because of Lazarus' death and the sorrow it caused. (John 11:32-36)

721. ACTS
722. AMOS
723. CHRONICLES
724. COLOSSIANS
725. CORINTHIANS
726. DANIEL
727. DEUTERONOMY
728. ECCLESIASTES
729. EPHESIANS
730. ESTHER
731. EXODUS
732. EZEKIEL
733. EZRA
734. GALATIANS
735. GENESIS
736. HABAKKUK
737. HEBREWS
738. JEREMIAH
739. JOB
740. JOEL
741. JOHN
742. JONAH
743. JOSHUA
744. JUDE
745. LAMENTATIONS
746. LUKE
747. MARK
748. MICAH
749. PETER
750. PSALMS
751. RUTH
752. SAMUEL
753. SONG OF SOLOMON
754. THESSALONIANS
755. TIMOTHY

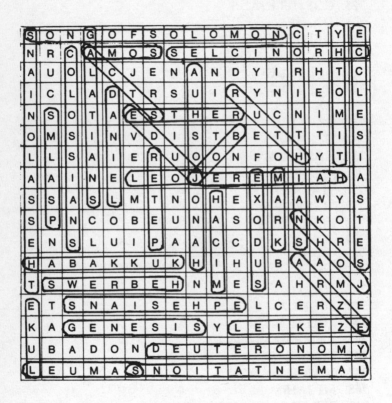

43. Multiple Choice—New Testament

756. B. (Matthew 13:55)
757. All four. (Matthew 26:65, 67; Mark 14:64, 65)
758. B. (Matthew 27:31; Mark 15:20)
759. C. (Matthew 17:1-3; Mark 9:2-4; Luke 9:28-30)
760. B. (Mark 9:41)
761. A. (Acts 4:18-20)
762. C. (Mark 4:36-38)
763. B. (Matthew 14:1-2)
764. B. (Luke 9:52-54)
765. D. (John 13:26, 30)
766. D. (Acts 13:14, 16, 33)
767. A. (Acts 21:28-29)
768. B. (2 John 1:1)
769. A. (Luke 2:43-46)
770. B. (Mark 2:23-24)
771. C. (Luke 1:13-19)
772. C. (Luke 2:8-9)
773. B. (John 3:27-29)
774. D. (John 4:49-50)
775. C. (Mark 15:25, 34-37)

44. The Last Letter

776. Rich. (Luke 19:2)
777. B. (Matthew 4:21; Mark 1:19; Luke 5:10)
778. Zedekiah. (Jeremiah 38:5-6)
779. C. (Genesis 29:24)
780. All were good friends of Job. (Job 2:11)
781. Zechariah. (9:9)
782. D. (Zechariah 11:7)
783. Zimri. (1 Kings 16:9-10, 15)
784. John the Baptist. (Luke 1:57, 60, 67)
785. The daughters of Zion. (Isaiah 3:16)

45. Final Potpourri

786. "Surely goodness and mercy shall follow me all the days of my life; and I will dwell in the house of the Lord for ever." (Psalms 23:6)

787. Both were born of previously barren women, after divine intercession. (Genesis 16:1; 17:19; 21:1-3; Samuel 1:2, 11, 19-20)

788. Both were married to Elkanah (1 Samuel 1:1-2)

789. Both were false gods served by the children of Israel. (Judges 10:6)

790. A. (Isaiah 10:22)

791. He was Noah, and that was the day "the windows of heaven were opened" and the Great Flood began. (Genesis 7:11)

792. A. (Judges 14:5-6; 1 Samuel 17:34-35; 1 Chronicles 11:22)

793. It's the entire Psalm 117, the shortest psalm of all. (Psalms 117:1-2)

794. Joshua and his soldiers; to march in a circle around the walled city of Jericho. (Joshua 6:2-4)

795. The Golden Rule: "Therefore all things whatsoever ye would that men should do to you, do ye even so to them: for this is the law and the prophets." (Matthew 7:12)